THE VEGETARIAN OPTION

Simple, vegetarian, delicious

SIMON HOPKINSON

Illustrations by Alice Pattullo

quadrille

Publishing Director Sarah Lavelle
Editor Susannah Otter
Design Manager Claire Rochford
Designer Katherine Keeble
Illustrator Alice Pattullo
Production Director Vincent Smith
Production Controller Tom Moore

This edition published in 2018 by Quadrille,
an imprint of Hardie Grant Publishing

Quadrille
52–54 Southwark Street
London SE1 1UN
quadrille.com

Cataloguing in Publication Data: a catalogue record for this book is available from the British Library.

ISBN 978 1 78713 2481
Printed in China

CONTENTS

INTRODUCTION

One evening in the late summer of 2007 and probably a Sunday, I found myself rummaging around in the salad drawer at the bottom of the fridge. Unusually for me, the interior was relatively bare, but all I wanted to eat, anyway, was a bowl of something quick to cook; not really substantial, though nourishing. Two items, slightly the worse for wear, caught my eye: a lone courgette not yet limp and a packet of ready-sliced runner beans, past their sell-by date by 3 days. There was also the remains of a bunch of parsley. So, I set to work.

I cut the courgette in half and then into long, thin strips (the most taxing chore of the entire assembly) to mimic the traditional cut of the beans. I briefly boiled both vegetables in salted water until tender, then drained and tossed them into a pan containing a little warming olive oil and sliced garlic. I added a healthy grinding of pepper, stirred everything about a bit and, finally, sprinkled over some of the parsley, finely chopped, and turned that through as well. Into a hot bowl it went and then out with a pair of chopsticks. I ate the dish in about 7 minutes flat, standing in the kitchen listening to The Archers.

I cannot begin to tell you how delicious this simple and thrifty affair was, although, I guess, it will not surprise you as there would have been little point in relating it. As I slipped the empty bowl – licked clean actually, it was just me – into a soapy sink, it occurred to me how the dish was all of itself. It did not need any accompaniment whatsoever, although I suppose a piece of good bread might have been better employed than my tongue, but, as I was attempting to not eat bread at the time, the bin was bare.

More importantly, however, was that I don't think I would have enjoyed it as much if there had been an accompaniment of a cut of meat, a slice of roast chicken, say, or even some lightly steamed fillets of sole. The dish was unique and perfect to that moment. Critically, it also allowed my thoughts to consider quite how easy and adaptable had been my little creation – if you can call it that – without the usual inclusion of my more usual, carnivorous desires.

I shall never be vegetarian. I cannot really see my culinary lifestyle drastically altering any time soon. I am absolutely not going to enter into the world of moral judgement here, I just love all foods. And together with the joy I am given by cooking them, the very idea of restriction of any kind would result in a life not worth living. Incidentally, my reference to 'loving all foods' isn't quite true. I do, I'm afraid, deeply loathe the Japanese fermented soy bean, known collectively as 'natto'. I am not even sure whether the most staunch vegetarian, virgin to such stinking slime, would countenance these either. But that is about the only comestible I would refuse to put in my mouth. Ironically, it is vegetarian food possibly at its most pure and healthy. Just filthy to eat, that's all. And it is handy to have a dish so readily available when asked of one: 'Is there anything you cannot eat?'

As with the delectable dish of courgettes and beans described above, my reasoning for this book is thus: dishes cooked without carnivorous and piscatorial leanings can be every bit as exciting as those with. This has nothing to do with a particular 'choice', which is why the title is qualified by one very important word: 'option'. In the restaurant business, this is the description applied to a dish that will be suitable for vegetarian clients. In my experience, this can be a last-minute request from the Head Chef to one of his team to 'come up with something...'. And, more often than not, that is exactly how the dish can read on occasional menus: stir-fried broccoli, tofu and oyster mushrooms with hazelnut oil might be one example. It may be nice for some, but it isn't for me.

At Bibendum this was never the case. That which was offered, however, was a thought-out selection of varying, regularly updated, seasonal dishes available from a completely separate, unadvertised menu. For example, when English asparagus came into season, it would always be there. A salad of green beans might have been another. In high summer there would be baked peppers with tomatoes and olive oil: 'Piedmontese peppers' – a dish with which Bibendum has always been associated – with the usual anchovy fillets eschewed for vegetarian guests. And there is a charming story to tell with reference to this.

There was once an American woman dining at the restaurant alone, a vegetarian, who demanded that all the dishes were explained to her in great detail (the à la carte menu is large, to say the least). Finally, she decided upon the Piedmontese peppers, but '... without the anchovies, please.' Graham Williams, then restaurant manager, complied with this easy request and dispatched the order to the chef in charge of first courses.

On this occasion, the kitchen failed to adhere to Graham's demands and sent out the dish complete with anchovy. The American woman, quite rightly, sent it back. We removed the anchovy and returned the peppers.

The lady tentatively asked 'And did you simply remove the anchovies?' Graham's reply was truthful to a tee. 'Well, I don't think I can eat this, as it is now tainted. I think I will have the risotto with white truffles instead.' 'Oh no', Graham expostulated, 'you can't possibly eat that. The truffles, at some point, would have been on the end of a pig's nose!' Quite possibly one of the best restaurant tales I know.

Now is the moment to discuss a few necessary guidelines that are useful to know whilst using this book.

There are several preparations that appear in certain recipes, which are used within other dishes, too. For instance: a spiced green paste (see page 152); a sesame paste (see page 169); a home-made ginger syrup (see page 89); an Indian masala paste (see page 52); an almond & jalapeño relish (see page 94).

As a general rule, use butter that is unsalted or, at least, slightly salted.

Salt is specified as either 'salt' (table salt) or 'Maldon' (sea salt).

Herbs are fresh unless otherwise stated.

Oven timings are for conventional ovens. If you are using a fan-assisted oven, reduce the temperature by 15°C (1 Gas mark). Use an oven thermometer to check the temperature.

As you will discover, generally I prefer white peppercorns to black. This, however, is entirely a matter for you – and they are not always readily available, either. Sometimes, there is also a sound reasoning as to using white: black specks in mayonnaise, however aromatic their flavour, will always look a bit grubby.

I have also used 'agar flakes' in place of the non-vegetarian leaf gelatine, and to great effect, I am pleased to say. Clearspring agar flakes are available from selected supermarkets and online [www.clearspring.co.uk].

Most of the cheeses used in the book contain the non-vegetarian rennet, but I am led to believe that in West Sussex, at Twineham Grange (available on Ocado), a vegetarian hard cheese exists, which, allegedly, is similar to Parmesan, although the powers that be in Parma, Italy would furiously countenance such a comparison. And, I guess they would be right. For any other vegetarian cheeses, I leave it up to you to search them out.

Finally, I have give one recipe for stock: a delicious vegetable bouillon. In all recipes I simply refer to 'stock', rather than specify as to which one.

The option, as ever, is yours.

Simon Hopkinson, April 2009

Bouillon

It was at Marc Meneau's L'Esperance in Saint-Père-sous-Vézelay, north Burgundy that I first tasted a fine vegetable 'bouillon'. It was high summer, around the end of July, 1985. The bouillon was poured at table, chilled – nay, ice-cold – into a shallow glass soup plate ready garnished with a dice of jewel-like vegetables. It was exactly what was needed after the journey from Paris in a hire car without air conditioning.

Well, I had never eaten anything like it! As Michelin had bestowed their coveted three stars upon the restaurant, I suppose one would have expected something startling. But quite how chef Meneau had managed to infuse such intensive flavour into that which resembled nothing more than a clear, pale yellow watery liquid was difficult to understand. I almost wanted to drink this elixir without interruption from the floating pieces of vegetable, it was so good.

The secret, I discovered, was to cook the bouillon in a sealed 'Le Parfait' preserving jar, and I do honestly believe that this method gives the best results. However, I have also experimented with a pressure cooker, for about

30 minutes, with good results, but the intensity of flavour here versus the original method is slightly less full and less clean tasting. I would suggest that if you are using the bouillon as the star of a dish, it is worth using the preserving jar method. Otherwise, traditionally simmer everything in a covered stainless steel pan on a very low heat, for about 1½ hours.

You may want a stronger flavoured bouillon for using in soups, sauces, a risotto, say, where clarity and finesse are less important. If so, I suggest that as you strain the stock through a fine sieve, you press as much juice from the vegetable debris with the back of a ladle as you can.

Conversely, for the finest clear vegetable bouillon, strain through a muslin-lined sieve and leave to drain without pressure. Even then, you may perceive the merest collection of base deposit. If so, simply allow the bouillon to settle and then carefully decant into another container, leaving the sediment behind.

The recipe overleaf uses the Meneau preserving jar method, but the choice of flavouring ingredients are mine.

My vegetable bouillon (stock)

Throughout the book, this bouillon will simply be referred to as 'stock'. In place of the salt, I have tried using the same 3 tsp of Marigold Swiss Vegetable Bouillon powder. This can be rewarding if you wish for more oomph in the final result. However, I think you can taste its presence so, if you are a purist, then just salt it is.

Makes about 1.5 litres

100g carrots, peeled and chopped
100g leeks, both green and white parts, chopped and well washed
100g celery, chopped
100g white button mushrooms, thinly sliced
250g white onion, peeled and chopped
200g ripe tomato, chopped
3 garlic cloves, halved
3 bay leaves
handful of parsley sprigs, roughly chopped
21 black peppercorns
3 tsp Maldon salt
about 1.5 litres water

You will need three scrupulously washed 750ml capacity 'Le Parfait' pre-serving jars, and to use a pan that is deep enough to take the jars and almost immerse them in water. It is worth placing a thickly folded sheet of newspaper in the bottom, or a small piece of cardboard underneath each jar, to prevent an, albeit rare, cracking of the glass. (I use a stove-top metal heat-diffuser as a trivet.)

Thoroughly mix the vegetables and tomato together in a roomy bowl. Now, half-fill the preserving jars with the vegetables and then equally distribute the garlic, herbs and peppercorns among them. Add the remaining vegetables and then add 1 tsp salt to each jar. Add the water, stopping about 2cm from the top. Seal the jars.

Place the jars in the pan and add cold water until it almost reaches the lids. Slowly bring up to a very gentle simmer, then cover and cook for 2 hours, topping up with boiling water from a kettle whenever the volume has visibly dropped. Once the 2 hours is up, allow the bouillon to cool completely in the water.

Either store until needed (keep in the fridge for safety, even though sterilised) or break the seal and strain the bouillon there and then. Discard the vegetables; they have done their work. Once strained, the bouillon may successfully be frozen in small, plastic pots.

VEGETABLES

Tomatoes & Olive Oil

The finest tomatoes I have ever had the pleasure of both using and eating are those locally grown in The Mani, on the Peloponnese peninsula in southern Greece. So heavy are these with sweet, fragrant flesh and juice, occasional fruits have weighed up to 750g each! Of course, simply sliced and dressed with olive oil (again local, naturally) they are at their most superb and beautiful to behold, with their sparkling seeds pocketed within thick, meaty partitions. I particularly enjoy eating them with some thinly sliced onions, which, in Greece, are a lovely pale pink, mild and sweet; plus the olive oil, of course. And, finally, my perfect breakfast is a thick slice of tomato, slowly fried in olive oil, with a fried egg (from the butcher's wife) popped on top. I call it 'my small Greek breakfast'.

Cooked, these gorgeous toms behave quite magnificently. The English friends who have invited me into their Greek holiday home enjoy a Bloody Mary as much as I do, so we make our own fresh tomato juice. The tomatoes, however, need to be slightly cooked, as simply making a purée of raw tomatoes will only give you a sort of pink pap. Given time, this would separate out into an unattractive suspension of pulp and pale, thin juice. So, core the tomatoes, blanch in boiling water for a few seconds and then peel (although not essential, I sometimes wonder if the skins contribute bitterness, once cooked). Cut them up into rough chunks and put into a large, stainless steel pan with a little salt and a pinch of sugar; if the tomatoes are naturally sweet then this will probably be unnecessary. Add a little water to start the cooking process and put on a low heat.

The trick here is to take the process only until the tomatoes have given off most of their juice, but still remain a touch undercooked. If heated too much, the juice tastes of cooked tomatoes, and again, once cooled and allowed to settle, it is liable to separate. Now, force the mixture through a coarse sieve using the back of a ladle, or, better still, a mouli-légumes (vegetable mill), then pass this through a finer sieve to remove the seeds. Job done. Keep in a screw-top bottle in the fridge, where it will stay fresh for 4–5 days. Shake well before use.

I buy my everyday olive oil from Garcia on Portobello Road. However, two very particular olive oils – one from Tuscany, the other from Provence – need special mention. The Italian one is Cappezana, from a medieval estate that has been producing olive oil since 804 AD. This I only ever use for fine dressings or spooning over thick slices of fresh mozzarella, or it's creamy cousin, burrata. I would also use it to dress the choicest sliced tomatoes, on the rare occasion that I may find them in West London, on a warm summer's day.

The French oil is from Le Moulin de Jean-Marie Cornille, in the village of Maussane-les-Alpilles, near St. Rèmy de Provence, but is generally known simply as Huile de Maussane. I know of no other oil as fragrantly pungent as this one, although it has a refinement and individuality that, for me, is unique. When used to fabricate golden aïoli, it is peerless.

Tomato jelly with basil & goat's cheese

Before writing this book, I had never needed to use a vegetarian gelling agent, namely agar-agar, although I knew vaguely of its seaweed origins, so highly prized in Japan. In Ireland, carragheen moss, a different variety of seaweed is used for the purpose, notably in the pudding known, not surprisingly, as Carragheen moss pudding. I had no idea of the setting properties of agar-agar or, clearly, how much to use. On using it, I discovered that the instructions on the packet gave a set that was very much too firm; well, for me, it was. I spent a great deal of time experimenting with the set, and the resultant, delicate texture achieved in the following recipe is one of enormous finesse, melting in the mouth in the nicest possible way. Agar flakes, however, will not produce a crystal clear jelly in the way conventional gelatine leaves do. Or, at least, they didn't for me. However, an agar jelly has the advantage that it does not form a skin. Note that it will eventually set at room temperature, too.

Serves 4

200ml stock
2 heaped tsp agar flakes
500g ripest tomatoes (cherry, small plum or very ripe summer tomatoes), finely chopped or processed to a mush
1 tsp Maldon salt
1 tsp sugar
pinch of dried chilli flakes
125g soft goat's cheese
1 heaped tbsp soured cream
1 small clove garlic, crushed to a paste with a little Maldon salt
small handful of basil leaves, chopped fine
freshly ground white pepper

Put the stock into a stainless steel pan, sprinkle over the agar flakes but do not stir in. Allow to come up to a gentle simmer and then swirl the pan around over the heat, until the flakes begin to melt. Simmer for 3–4 minutes and then add the tomatoes, salt, sugar and chilli. Bring up to just under simmering point and then pass through a fine sieve suspended over a bowl. Initially, simply allow the juice to drip through, then carefully move the tomato pulp around with a spoon to coax more juice out, but do not force or press it.

Meanwhile, thoroughly mix the goat's cheese, soured cream, garlic, basil and pepper together in a bowl. Spoon into the base of four small glass beakers (or similar), dividing it equally.

Now take the bowl of tomato liquid and place it over a larger bowl filled with ice cubes and water. Taking a metal spoon, gently stir the liquid around until it just begins to gel; about 10 minutes, but note that when it starts to gel, it will happen quite swiftly.

Spoon the jelly over the cheese mixture and place in the fridge to set for about 1 hour – the jellies are best eaten there and then. Serve with teaspoons and eat with thin, hot buttered toast. An elegant summer first course, eaten out of doors.

Tomato salad with basil cream dressing & olive oil

I first recall eating tomato salad with a cream dressing at the Italian restaurant Montpeliano, in London's Knightsbridge. It must have been in the late 1970s, soon after I had first arrived in London. When the salad arrived, we were somewhat surprised to receive two large white plates covered with ripest red, sliced tomatoes, anointed with a generous dressing of what looked like double cream. That was until we tasted it. Ice cold and almost sweet and sour, this cream dressing was just fabulous. Freshly torn basil leaves, a grinding of pepper from the handsome waiter (giant mills all the rage, then) and a trickle of good olive oil shining in rivulets upon its creamy surface... Just perfect.

Serves 2

1 ½ tbsp white wine vinegar
2 tbsp warm water
Maldon salt and freshly ground pepper
75ml whipping cream
50ml extra virgin olive oil, plus a little extra
pinch of sugar
7–8 basil leaves, torn or chopped
4 ripe, medium tomatoes, cored and sliced

In a mixing bowl, whisk together the wine vinegar, water and seasoning until combined. Now whisk in the cream, olive oil and sugar until well amalgamated, then stir in the basil.

Lay the tomatoes onto a large plate (preferably white), very lightly season and spoon over the dressing. Trickle over a little extra olive oil and serve directly.

Baked stuffed tomatoes 'paella style'

Although the flavours in this dish are those of Spanish paella, the rice I have chosen is Italian carnaroli; other risotto rice may be employed (a simple arborio or vialone nano), but I find carnaroli swells more evenly and tenderly for the stuffing.

These tomatoes may also be served alongside other small dishes as part of a buffet lunch (in which case, one each is sufficient). For a first course, as here, you will need two.

Serves 4

8 firm, ripe medium tomatoes
½ small green pepper, de-seeded, pith removed and coarsely chopped
4 garlic cloves, peeled and crushed
large pinch of dried chilli
handful of flat parsley leaves
1 tsp Spanish paprika
1 tsp saffron threads, steeped in 1 tbsp boiling water
125ml olive oil, plus a little more, if liked
75g carnaroli rice
Maldon salt and freshly ground pepper

Remove the stalks from the tomatoes and then turn them over. Using a small, sharp knife, slice through about a fifth of the way down the tomato, to give little caps. Reserve these for later. Now, using a teaspoon, carefully scoop out all of the tomato innards into a bowl. Place the hollowed-out shells in a roasting dish that will accommodate them snugly.

Put the green pepper, garlic, chilli, parsley, paprika and infused saffron (with its water) into a food processor and pulse until the ingredients are evenly but coarsely chopped. Now tip in the tomato pulp with 100ml of the olive oil and process further until the entire mixture is a sloppy, seedy and oily tomato pap, with the other solids now more finely processed and in suspension.

Put the rice into the bowl that previously held the tomato pulp and pour over the tomato pap from the food processor. Mix well and season with salt to taste. Leave to soak for 30 minutes, stirring occasionally. Preheat the oven to 200°C/gas mark 6.

Fill the tomatoes with the rice mixture. Don't be tempted to over-fill – there may be a little left over – but do make sure that as much liquid as possible is included, even if it overflows into the dish. Replace the little caps onto the tomatoes and trickle over the remaining oil (plus a little more, if you like).

Bake in the oven for about 45 minutes, turning the heat down a touch if the tomatoes are browning too much – but browned and blistered they certainly must be! Taste a little of the rice to make sure it is fully cooked, although it will also continue to swell and tenderise as it cools. Serve at room temperature, for preference, basting well with the juices and oil just before serving.

Homemade tomato sauce

Always good to have to hand... and it freezes well, too.

Makes about 1 litre
2kg ripe tomatoes, peeled
1 head of garlic, each clove peeled and then bruised
2 bay leaves
leaves from 1 head of green celery, or 2 celery sticks, chopped
thinly pared rind of 1 small lemon
2 tsp sugar
a little salt

Roughly chop the tomatoes and put them into a heavy-bottomed pan. Add all the other ingredients and bring to a simmer. Allow to cook very, very gently for 1½–2 hours, stirring from time to time. As the final sauce consistency should be a bit sloppy and still just pourable, take the pan from the heat before the sauce looks too thick.

Personally, I like to first use a vegetable mill (mouli-légumes) using the finest disk and then further force the resultant sauce through a fine sieve, pressing down well with the back of a small ladle.

Asparagus & Artichokes

When they overlap, this pair is one of the great green treats of early summer. At Secretts Farm [www.secretts.co.uk], near Godalming, Surrey, on a sunny Saturday morning, you can often find me striding between the well-kept rows of asparagus spears, with trusty sharp knife and basket. I am like a child indulging in a brand new craze over and over again, and love this excellent place for allowing me this simple pleasure. And there is a further bonus on the way back from the asparagus beds – a giant allotment given over to globe artichokes. Joy of joys!

A few years back, and for a couple of years, or so, Secretts had to call a halt to pick-your-own asparagus as a significant number of pickers had, how shall we say, been unscrupulous with their cutting skills – or lack of, I guess. This ignorant behaviour involved simply cutting off the asparagus tips, rather than removing entire spears, as more thoughtful and respectful pickers are moved to do. Mind you, it is how most asparagus – especially those out of season – are sold in supermarkets. Perhaps that is all these bewildered folk know.

I see choosing and picking my own asparagus as not just a joy, but the choicest luxury, and like to pick the biggest, fattest spears. To be deprived of such a brief, seasonal pleasure is saddening. So, please be kind and respectful of this excellent enterprise – and of the asparagus, too – so it may continue year in, year out.

Traditionally cut asparagus should include the white base beneath the soil. Once well washed, these may be used along with the peel from the stalks to make wonderful asparagus soups – to be enjoyed both hot and chilled. Rice is the most successful thickener here, as potatoes can sometimes produce a gluey texture. A good asparagus soup should be limpidly smooth, a lovely pale green (from the skins added late in the cooking process) and just a touch of cream added as a final enrichment. Tarragon or chervil are good herbs to employ as secondary flavours.

A final thought concerning asparagus. There are those who insist that English asparagus is the finest in the world. I think it is wonderful too, but I would argue that all asparagus, absolutely freshly picked anywhere in the world and plunged promptly into a pan of fast-boiling salted water to cook for several minutes, will taste just as fine. Freshness, with asparagus, is all.

The artichokes grown at Secretts are the large, Breton variety, rather than the smaller, softer and purple-leafed variety most synonymous with Italy – and the Veneto, in particular. Here, in March and April, there are tiny artichokes in the Rialto market harvested from the islands of the lagoon. These are known as castraure, which literally translates as 'taken out from' (with connotations of castration).

The first tiny bud is cut out from the very centre of the plant, allowing future, larger artichokes to flourish through the summer –as many as twenty per plant. They are not cheap, but such a short season never is. At Harry's Bar, six are trimmed to the size of small corks, baked with olive oil and simply served warm on a small plate. So delicious they are, I eat them very slowly using my fingers, while momentarily forgetting that they might possibly cost the price of ten pizzas, the other side of San Marco. Then again, what would I want with ten pizzas?

Warm asparagus custards with tarragon vinaigrette

The texture of these little darlings is wonderfully wobbly and delicate, so do take the greatest care when the moment of optimum set is reached. Practice makes perfect, as with all crucial cookery lore.

Serves 4

for the custards
250g asparagus
salt
a little soft butter for greasing the ramekins
2 large eggs
2 large egg yolks
125ml whipping cream
Maldon salt and freshly ground white pepper

for the vinaigrette
1 tbsp tarragon vinegar
1 tsp Dijon mustard
salt and freshly ground pepper
2 tbsp sunflower oil
3 tbsp extra virgin olive oil
2 tsp finely chopped tarragon leaves

Trim the stalk ends of the asparagus and peel the lower part of the stems, then cut the spears into short lengths. Cook them in boiling, well-salted water until a touch more than just tender, drain and immediately plunge into a bowl of water chilled with plenty of ice cubes. Leave until quite cold, then lift out and carefully, but thoroughly, dry in a tea towel. The asparagus will then be ready to use. The drained, cooked weight should hover around the 200g mark.

Preheat the oven to 150°C/gas mark 2. Butter four ramekins and line the base of each with a tiny disc of greaseproof paper.

Put the cooked asparagus into a blender with the eggs and egg yolks and purée until really smooth. Pour into a fine sieve suspended over a bowl and, with aid of a small ladle, force through as much mixture as possible. Stir the cream into the purée until well mixed and season with a little salt and pepper to taste. Pour the mixture into the prepared ramekins, filling them to just below the brim.

Cover each with a round of foil and place in a deep baking dish. Pour tap-hot water into the dish until it comes at least three-quarters of the way up the sides of the moulds. Bake in the oven for 25–30 minutes, or until just firm to the touch. Leave to cool until warm, but no cooler.

Meanwhile, make the vinaigrette. Simply mix together the vinegar, mustard and seasoning in a small bowl, then whisk in the oils until emulsified (add a tiny splash of hot water to aid this, if you like). Stir in the tarragon.

To serve, spoon a little of the vinaigrette onto the surface of each custard. Eat with fingers of hot buttered toast.

Asparagus with olive oil & blood orange butter sauce

The dressing here is an oily version of the butter-rich sauce known as 'Maltaise'. Unusually diverting.

Serves 2

1 large bunch of asparagus (about 14–16 spears)
salt

for the sauce

2 large egg yolks
grated zest and juice of 2 blood oranges
75g unsalted butter, melted and kept warm
75ml extra virgin olive oil
salt and freshly ground white pepper
squeeze of lemon juice, to taste

To make the sauce, place the egg yolks in a glass bowl with the orange juice and zest and suspend the bowl over a pan of barely simmering water, making sure it is not touching the water. Whisk over the heat for several minutes until the mixture is thick and glossy; be careful to not overcook it or the eggs will scramble.

Remove from the heat and slowly whisk in the butter until incorporated, leaving behind the milky residue for the time being; if the finished sauce is too thick, some of this may later be added to thin it slightly. Now whisk in the olive oil, season and add the lemon juice. The consistency of the sauce should be similar to a loose mayonnaise – pourable, yet wobbly. Strain the sauce through a fine sieve into a warmed bowl (to rid the sauce of the orange zest).

Trim the asparagus bases and peel the lower end of the stalks. Add to a pan of boiling well-salted water and boil for about 5 minutes, or until tender when pierced with a sharp knife. Please don't undercook the asparagus, as I think there is nothing worse; the spears should just give to the teeth. Once cooked, lift them out with a slotted spoon and drain on a tea towel. Divide between two warm plates and hand the sauce separately at table.

Warm salad of asparagus & new potatoes

A pleasure of both texture and seasonality is the general idea, here.

Serves 4

350g small Jersey potatoes, scrupulously scraped or peeled
salt
2 large mint sprigs
25g unsalted butter
250g asparagus tips
hearts of 2 round lettuces, leaves separated, washed and carefully dried
Maldon salt
2 hard-boiled eggs, shelled
handful of chervil sprigs

for the butter sauce

juice of 1 lemon
pinch of caster sugar
75g cold unsalted butter, cut into small chunks
freshly ground white pepper
1 tbsp snipped chives

Simmer the potatoes in lightly salted water just to cover, with the mint, until tender. Drain over another pan or bowl, keep the water for now, and return the potatoes to the pan with the butter. Stir together, cover and keep warm.

For the sauce, take a roomy and shallow, stainless steel or enamelled saucepan and squeeze in the lemon juice. Add 6 tbsp of the potato cooking water and the sugar, then simmer this mixture until reduced by half. Now slowly incorporate the butter, one chunk at a time, whisking over a thread of heat until limpid and homogenous (this is essentially a light butter sauce). Season with pepper. Again, keep warm.

Peel the asparagus tips from just below the bud and slice them in half lengthways. Add to a pan of boiling well-salted water and boil rapidly for about 1–2 minutes (eat one to see if they are cooked; they should be just tender, not almost raw), then drain.

Slice the warm potatoes and add these, together with the asparagus, to the butter sauce. Turn gently through the sauce with the chives, until all are evenly coated.

Arrange the lettuce leaves on four plates and divide the asparagus and potatoes between them. Sprinkle with a little Maldon salt and judiciously grate over the egg. Generously scatter over chervil sprigs, which are not there just to look pretty; their faint aniseed flavour is very pleasing, here.

Asparagus frittata with soft cheese & chives

This would be a fine opportunity to use asparagus spears known as 'sprue', which are much thinner and, consequently, less expensive than more perfect specimens. If so, do not bother to peel them, just remove the tougher base stalks.

Serves 2

200g asparagus
1 tbsp olive oil
salt and cayenne pepper
scant scraping of freshly grated nutmeg
3 large eggs, beaten
125g soft cream cheese
30g Parmesan, finely grated
2 tsp snipped chives
a thin slice of butter

Trim the asparagus bases, peel the lower end of the stalks and thinly slice the spears on the diagonal. Warm the olive oil in a non-stick frying pan, add the asparagus and season with salt, cayenne pepper and nutmeg. Cook gently over a low heat until the asparagus are tender and very lightly coloured; eat a sliver to see if it is cooked through. Tip out onto a plate, set aside and wipe out the frying pan.

In a mixing bowl, beat together the eggs, cream cheese, Parmesan and chives until smooth. Return the frying pan to a moderate heat, add the butter and heat until just beginning to froth. Pour in the egg mixture, turn down the heat to low and then quietly begin to bring in the frothing edges to the liquid centre of the pan using a spatula or palette knife.

Now, tip in the cooked asparagus and carefully disperse evenly. Continue to gently lift the more cooked parts of the frittata, so allowing the liquid egg to slip underneath until a happy, soft and curd-like medium has evolved – this should take no more than 2 minutes, or so.

Slide the frittata onto a plate and eat warm or at room temperature, but certainly not hot from the pan.

Globe artichoke, broad bean & pea stew

Do not be concerned as to the dull green look of the finished dish. This is what happens when such vegetables are given a slow-cooked treatment.

Serves 4
4–5 tbsp extra virgin
olive oil
150g spring onions, trimmed and sliced
2–3 garlic cloves, peeled and sliced
1 tsp fennel seeds, crushed slightly with a pestle and mortar
3 tbsp dry vermouth
200g artichoke hearts (fresh or frozen), cut into small wedges
200g podded broad beans
200g shelled peas
75ml water
salt and freshly ground pepper
2 tbsp chopped mint
squeeze of lemon juice (optional)

Warm 2–3 tbsp of the olive oil in a solid, roomy pot. Add the spring onions, garlic and fennel seeds and gently soften until translucent and limp. Pour in the vermouth, allow to bubble for a minute or two, then put in the artichoke hearts. Cover and allow to stew over a low heat for about 15–20 minutes, stirring occasionally.

Now add the broad beans and peas with another 1 tbsp olive oil and continue to cook, covered, for a further 5 minutes. Add the water, seasoning and another 1 tbsp of oil and stir all together. Cover with a circle of greaseproof paper, put on the lid and continue stewing, very, very gently, until the vegetables are well cooked and no longer bright green. Only now, is the dish almost ready. It is important that the vegetables should be well cooked; it is a stew, after all. Reckon on about 45–50 minutes gentle cooking time, in all.

Now add the mint and, if you like, the lemon juice. Spoon into a handsome serving dish (preferably white), adding just a trickle more oil over the surface. Serve at room temperature to enjoy the dish at its best.

Globe artichoke soup with black truffles

Consider making this soup only if you have access to ready-prepared artichoke hearts, either frozen (available from selected supermarkets), or fresh if you happen to be staying in Italy – almost always there will be a vendor in the local market with trays of prepared artichoke hearts bobbing about in acidulated water he will gladly sell you. Choose the cheapest ones available, as they vary in price from perfect to off-cuts. Clearly, here, the latter will be perfect.

The flavour of the soup is impeccable in its delicacy and may, of course, be consumed without the luxury of thin shavings of black truffle over its surface, once decanted into warmed, shallow soup plates. There again, the wider the plate, the greater the area of possible abundance. So, if you are lucky enough to have access to such rare bounty, shave away willy-nilly.

Serves 4

2 tbsp olive oil
200g leeks, trimmed, sliced and washed
500g artichoke hearts (fresh or frozen), chopped
2 garlic cloves, crushed and chopped
salt and freshly ground white pepper
500ml stock
350ml milk
50g butter
75ml whipping cream
fresh black truffle (optional)

Heat the olive oil in a roomy pan, add the leeks and stew until softened. Add the artichokes and garlic, stir around for a few moments, then season and pour in the stock and milk. Bring up to a simmer, cover and cook gently for about 30–40 minutes, or until the artichokes are very tender and almost falling apart. Do not worry about the split appearance of the liquid, it will be resolved at the next stage.

Now process the mixture in a blender until very smooth indeed. Pass through a fine sieve back into the (wiped-clean) pan and then whisk in the butter and cream, while keeping the soup hot over a medium heat. Once all is ready and velvety smooth, pour into heated soup plates and thinly shave over some black truffle – or not, as the case may be.

Cauliflower & Broccoli

When a freshly harvested cauli is in the peak of condition I gain great pleasure in running my hand over its creamy white curds, almost completely enclosed by sturdy, green leafy ribs, still wet with rainwater or morning dew. Granted, it is only at the very best farm shops where this is ever likely to happen, but the experience is a special one – well, it is for me. There is always something wonderful when encountering really fresh produce – be it organic or otherwise – and the cauliflower takes some beating in this respect.

Maybe this is because cauliflower is often seen as something rather mundane in the panoply of 'world' vegetables that are now so readily available to most of us. Often, in fact, the more ordinary the produce the more I become excited when I discover it in excellent nick.

To carefully prise apart crisp florets of the freshest cauli and turn them into a deliciously comforting cauliflower cheese (see page 34), is one of the nicest initial preparations, particularly when one knows that, once boiled until just tender, they are going to be blanketed in the very best cheese sauce one can possibly muster. All such thrills matter to the caring cook who loves to eat good things.

Dear old broccoli is no different in its ubiquity, except that it appears in more varied guises. Pile upon pile of purple sprouting broccoli is the treat of mid-February into mid-April – the native harvest, that is. Some years ago I was staying on the Suffolk coast and made a slight detour to Alder Carr Farmers' Market, just on the edge of the village of Needham Market [www.aldercarrfarm.co.uk], on my route back to London.

My arrival happily coincided with a tractor returning from the land with a truck attached that was, astonishingly, laden with what looked like an entire field of purple sprouting broccoli. Although there was plenty of broccoli in the market, I excitedly insisted that I would like mine fresh from the tractor. Eager to please this grown-up child, they duly allowed me to choose my bounty. Naturally, I purchased roughly four times the amount I actually needed. So, both parties satisfied.

To briefly return to those cauliflowers, one of the most delicious, almost-instant soups may be made using small florets of cauli. Quickly boil them in a lightly flavoured stock until really quite soft, together with several thinly sliced spring onions, white part only. Add a knob of butter then whiz in a blender until super-smooth. Strain through a fine sieve and serve in piping hot soup bowls, with a spoonful or two of cream floated on the surface. The fresh taste of this lily-white soup is especially fine and should not be reheated. Eat with tiny, buttery croûtons.

Cauliflower cheese

Personally, I generally use tasty Lancashire for my cauli cheese, as that is what my Mother always bought from Bury market. But any good, firm British cheese will do fine, such as Cheddar or Caerphilly.

Serves 2, generously

1 cauliflower
salt and freshly ground white pepper
500ml full-cream milk
2 cloves
1 small onion, peeled and chopped
1 bay leaf
75g butter
50g plain flour
a little freshly grated nutmeg
200g firm cheese, grated, plus a little extra for sprinkling on top

Remove the green leaves from the cauliflower and break the curds into roughly even-sized florets. Add the cauliflower florets to a pan of boiling salted water and boil until almost tender (remember, they will continue to cook whilst in the sauce, in the oven). Drain and lay out on a folded tea towel; their cooking water will continue to exude for quite some minutes after draining. Preheat the oven to 190°C/gas mark 5. Put the milk, cloves, onion and bay leaf in a small saucepan and bring up to a simmer. Cook for a minute or two, then cover and leave to infuse off the heat for 10 minutes, or so.

In another pan, melt the butter and stir in the flour. Cook, stirring, over a low heat for a few minutes, then remove from the heat and strain in the hot milk all in one go. Whisk together vigorously until well amalgamated. Using a wooden spoon, stir continuously until the sauce begins to thicken and become very smooth. Leave to cook for a further 10 minutes over the merest heat. Add the cheese and stir until it has fully melted into the sauce. Season with pepper and nutmeg and taste for salt.

Place the cauliflower in an ovenproof dish that will accommodate it snugly. Carefully pour over the sauce so that it fully coats each floret and sprinkle with the extra cheese. Bake in the oven for a good 25–30 minutes, or until the surface is well blistered and the sauce is bubbling nicely around the edges.

Purple sprouting broccoli with sauce courchamps

A most delicious sauce, this one, and adapted from a recipe in Elizabeth David's *An Omelette and a Glass of Wine*. Unique and unusual, it is not the same if you forgo the anisette. Although only available in a large bottle, it keeps for ages.

Serves 2

12 purple sprouting broccoli stalks, well trimmed
salt

for the sauce

2–3 bushy tarragon sprigs
3–4 parsley sprigs
2 shallots, peeled and coarsely chopped
freshly ground pepper
1 tsp smooth Dijon mustard
2 tsp anisette de Bordeaux
juice of ½ small lemon
2 tsp light soy sauce
4 tbsp extra virgin olive oil, plus more if needed

Cook the broccoli in boiling salted water until tender. For the sauce, pick the leaves from the herb sprigs and place them in a small blender with all the other ingredients. Purée until smooth. Taste the sauce and see if you need any more of anything. Pour into a small serving bowl. Drain the broccoli and serve, using fingers to dip the stalks in the sauce.

Broccoli with chopped egg & sherry breadcrumbs

Sharp, buttery and crunchy textures. A surprisingly comforting assembly.

Serves 2

80g butter
40g fresh white breadcrumbs
salt and freshly ground pepper
2 tbsp Amontillado sherry
1 large head of broccoli, broken up into small florets
2 hard-boiled eggs, chopped (or grated, if you like)
1 ½ tbsp sherry vinegar

Heat 40g of the butter in a pan until frothing and add the breadcrumbs, salt and pepper. Fry gently until all the butter has been soaked up and allow to colour for a few minutes, then pour in the sherry. Once the frothing has subsided, you will notice that the mixture has become all claggy. Don't worry, just turn down the heat and stir fairly constantly with a wooden spoon until lumps begin to collect. In time, about 15 minutes, these will break back down into crumbs, the sherry having been driven off by evaporation – its flavour left behind with the browned butter. The crumbs should be crisp and golden. Keep them warm.

Boil the broccoli in salted water until tender and drain well. Pile neatly into a hot serving dish and strew over the crumbs and chopped egg. Heat the remaining 40g of butter in a small pan until it begins to turn golden and smell nutty. Remove from the heat, wait a few seconds and then spoon in the vinegar, which will froth and splutter. Swirl the fat and liquid together to loosely amalgamate and then spoon over the broccoli. Serve without delay.

Pumpkin & Squash

I would reckon that many pumpkins sold in Britain remain uneaten, as they are only ever really seen in greengrocers – and supermarkets, most definitely – in the weeks leading up to Hallowe'en. Then again, I may be wrong. But, at this festive occasion, they are first emptied of their flesh (consumed?... I think not), a spooky face cut into the tough skin and a small candle placed inside. This is certainly not the case in the United States. While sales of pumpkin must also surely rocket during the month of October, with similar faces cut into their tough skin, pumpkins are also hugely popular at the American table, as well as flickering on the windowsill.

However, that which seems to be the most prevalent dish made from pumpkin in the United States has always been a problem, with me. That Pie. I just don't understand it. I can only hope that one day some extraordinarily brilliant American cook will present me with a slice of one that, at least, I can finish. I have mentioned elsewhere in this book how something deliciously bland will be just what one feels like eating from time to time. But when something is bland and tasteless and with a filling that has a texture similar to day-old wallpaper paste, I choose to pass. Perhaps I have just been unlucky, every single time.

Be that as it may, I love lots of American food. Maryland crab cakes, oysters Rockefeller, shad roe in early Spring, fabulous juicy steaks, southern fried chicken, pastrami on rye, lox and bagels are all wonderful. Then there is the irresistible fudgey-textured New York cheese-cake, the one that is 'clarty' – a Lancashire expression to describe food that sticks to the roof of your mouth. And, of course, the truly scrummy pecan pie. Now that is a pie which forgives all and everything.

I came to like squash – and butternut in particular – relatively late in my culinary life. To be honest, I gave it the same short shrift as pumpkin. I recall the other pumpkin recipe that I was always polite about and consumed dutifully. It was a soup that Mum used to make occasionally towards the end of her life. I never knew quite why she bothered, as it was forever and absolutely bereft of taste. Curious, that, as all her other dishes rarely failed to delight.

Anyway, squash is good. Baked butternut doused with olive oil and dressed with lemon juice (see page 37) is simple and delicious. The ravioli derivative that follows (on page 38) takes a little more time and effort, but is well worth the journey. And the pumpkin soup (overleaf) might just convince you that there is more to this vegetable than Hallowe'en lanterns.

Pumpkin soup 'Paul Bocuse'

I first encountered this curious, slightly hit-and-miss recipe in the back pages of the seminal book *Great Chefs of France*, by Quentin Crewe and Anthony Blake (tragically now out of print). It is the only book I have ever read cover to cover in one sitting – or one lying, in fact, as I devoured it through the night. Here is the original, word for word, as part of Bocuse's annual New Year greetings cards sent to friends:

Soupe de courge à la crème

'The pumpkin is a vegetable which it is wrong to neglect. One can make gratins and soup with it. Here is a delicious recipe. Cut the top off a 4–5 kilo pumpkin so that it looks like a soup bowl. Scoop out the seeds and three-quarters fill the pumpkin with alternate layers of grilled croûtons and grated Gruyère. Add salt and pepper and fill up the pumpkin with cream. Put in a hot oven for 2 hours and then put it on the table. There detach the flesh of the pumpkin with a spoon. Then stir with a ladle to mix the flesh with the soup and serve.'

Well, over the years I have played around with this, but have never used a giant pumpkin of the size the great Bocuse suggests. Also, although I have found the inclusion of croûtons can make the soup too thick, there have been times when simply seasoned cream and Gruyère appears too thin. However, the end result, using the latter method, is quite delicious when scoops of softened pumpkin flesh are stirred into its stringy curds. Whether one should call it a soup, or a 'baked pumpkin with cheese and cream', is debatable; a recipe to play with, I feel. Either way, bonne chance!, as chef might say... The above is my humble, adapted effort.

Serves about 4

1 small pumpkin, about 1.75–2kg
400ml double cream
1 garlic clove, peeled and chopped
salt and freshly ground pepper
150g Gruyère, or Beaufort if you like, freshly grated

Preheat the oven to 200°C/gas mark 6. Cut off the top quarter of the pumpkin to make a lid and set aside. Scoop out the seeds and stringy membrane using a spoon. Heat the cream with the garlic and seasoning almost to a simmer, then take off the heat, cover and leave to infuse for 20 minutes.

Strain the infused cream into the pumpkin cavity. Mix in the cheese, put on the lid and place in a roasting tin. Bake for 1½–2 hours, until the pumpkin flesh is tender when pierced with a fork and the outer skin of the pumpkin is nicely burnished; you may wish to turn the heat down slightly if the skin is becoming too brown.

Baked butternut squash with olive oil & lemon

This recipe is, of course, quite delicious in its own right: the baked squash flesh scooped from the skin into warmed, shallow bowls and dressed with lemon juice – plus a sprinkling of Parmesan if you like. The cooked flesh may also be used to make ravioli (see opposite).

Serves 4

about 1kg butternut squash
salt and freshly ground pepper
3–4 tbsp olive oil
lemon juice
freshly grated Parmesan, to serve (optional)

Preheat the oven to 190°C/gas mark 5. Quarter the squash lengthways and scoop out all seeds and stringy membrane. Place in a baking dish, season and generously spoon over olive oil. Bake for about 1 hour, basting occasionally, until the squash is very tender when pierced with a fork. Squeeze over lemon juice to taste. Serve hot, with Parmesan, if you like.

Squash ravioli with pine kernels, butter & sage

The baked butternut squash recipe should yield about 400g flesh, the quantity needed here. A hand-cranked pasta machine is fairly essential, unless you are an adept rolling-pin pasta maker.

Serves 6, as a first course

for the ravioli filling

1 onion, peeled and finely chopped
1 tbsp olive oil (from baking the squash, if there is some left)
25g butter
400g cooked butternut squash flesh, chopped
2 paper-wrapped amaretti biscuits (4 halves), crushed
2 heaped tbsp freshly grated Parmesan
1 large egg yolk
1 tbsp fresh white breadcrumbs
salt and freshly ground pepper

for the pasta

250g '00' pasta flour
2 large egg yolks
2 large eggs
1 tsp Maldon salt
extra beaten egg, for sealing the ravioli

to dress the pasta

large knob of butter
handful of sage leaves
handful of pine kernels
freshly grated Parmesan

To make the ravioli filling, fry the onion in the olive oil until golden and soft. Tip into a food processor and add the remaining filling ingredients. Process until fairly smooth, but not to a complete paste. Scoop out into a bowl, cover with cling film and set aside.

For the pasta, mix the ingredients together in a bowl until a firm dough is achieved (an electric food mixer with a flat beater, or dough hook, makes the task immeasurably easier). Knead for several minutes, wrap in cling film and allow to rest in the fridge for at least 30 minutes.

Take about one sixth of the pasta and start to feed it between the rollers of the pasta machine. Take the dough up to about level 4 to begin with, then fold it over like a business letter, turn it through 45° and then return to the first level. Try to do this three times; I believe this repetition gives a more supple pasta, that is more tender and giving once cooked. Take the pasta up to its thinnest level (7, on my machine), lay out the sheet on a floured surface and leave it to settle for a minute or two.

Now, place small teaspoonfuls of the squash mixture along the top half of the pasta sheet at, say, 6cm intervals. Lightly brush the pasta with egg in between the little mounds of filling and along the top edge of the sheet. Cut through from top to bottom between the filling mounds, making rectangles.

To form the ravioli, fold the lower part of each rectangle onto the upper part, enclosing the blob of filling. Seal carefully using your fingertips, taking care not to trap air within. Repeat with the rest of the pasta and filling, to make about 30 large ravioli in total.

To cook the ravioli, add to a pan of boiling salted water and boil gently for 4–5 minutes, or until tender. Lift one out to check it is cooked; when pinched with the fingers the edges should easily give to the touch.

Meanwhile, for the dressing, melt the butter in a small frying pan and add the sage leaves and pine kernels. Cook slowly, stirring occasionally, until the sage leaves become crisp and the pine kernels are golden. Drain the ravioli and divide among warmed bowls. Spoon over the warm dressing and sprinkle with Parmesan.

Cabbage & Chard

I was not a difficult child when it came to eating my greens. In fact, I can only remember one occasion when something Mum cooked, that I did not like, reappeared for supper. Mind you, it can't have been that terrible, as I now cannot for the life of me recall what it was. But greens it would never have been.

I always adored servings of soft and buttery, well-peppered cabbage. The varieties we ate – and those which I prefer to this day – are either the light green and pointy cabbage (hispi, I think, is its correct nomenclature) or the firmer, paler and sort of round-towards-oval shaped cabbage, which is nowhere near as huge and hard as the big brute – sometimes called Dutch – that is used for making coleslaw. Our cabbage was properly cooked, too.

Either cabbage should be trimmed and cut – including the core – into quarters, or sixths if large. Boil in generously salted water until just tender, then drain. Lay the cabbage on a tea towel and allow to cool a little. Now place on a chopping board, cut away the core and slice the leaves into large pieces. Return to the pan, add as much butter and pepper as you dare, then gently reheat and allow to very gently stew for 4–5 minutes, stirring occasionally. I hope you will agree with me that the result is supremely fine, hot buttered cabbage.

Of Savoy, the dark green crinkled one, I have never been much of a fan. There is always something slightly bitter within, together with a slight, sulphurous quality that displeases me. I know that many will not agree; my cookery friend Rowley Leigh in particular, with such disagreements being nothing new, but always in the kindest, most interested, way.

I know hardly anything at all about cavalo nero, the more recent darling of the newer, rustic kitchen (a contradiction in terms, but undeniably apt). I have never cooked this long and deeply dark green leafed Italian cabbage, but thoroughly enjoyed its almost stygian strands within its happiest home: a deep bowlful of ribollita, the 're-boiled', gorgeous thick soup so beloved of all Tuscans. That which is served at The River Café in West London, is one of the finest I have eaten.

Chard – or Swiss chard, to give it its full name – is a most useful and interesting plant, cookery wise, as it offers the opportunity to make two completely different dishes from the one vegetable. The glossy and deeply veined dark green leaves may be trimmed away from the fleshy stalks (sharp scissors are good, here). The leaves are best coarsely shredded and cooked simply in butter or olive oil. The stalks are at their finest, I think, when washed, trimmed and cut into short lengths, then steamed or boiled, laid in a shallow dish and covered with a light cheese sauce and baked as a gratin. Delicious. Please do try the recipe (on page 45).

Finally, Korean kimchi (on page 42) is not for the faint hearted, but it is undeniably good for those who, how shall we say, enjoy their food particularly perky – and also have the patience to wait. Read on…

Korean kimchi

This is adapted from a recipe in *Foods from the Far East,* by Bruce Cost, first published in the United States about 20 years ago. One of my favourite cookery books, it should be essential reading for all those interested in cooking with Asian ingredients.

Bruce's far-reaching Asian menu at Monsoon, his restaurant in San Francisco, was diverse – the kitchen producing remarkable dishes of great delicacy, yet with a heat, spice and freshness that made them unique.

Try to find a room in your home that you don't mind becoming quite pongy during the making of kimchi!

The fermentation period (the pongy period) should not be done out of doors unless, I guess, if it is warm weather. I once tried doing this outside in winter and the process slowed right down to almost nothing. Under the stairs might be better, perhaps?

In Korea, kimchi is eaten every single day, particularly at breakfast time, I understand.

Makes about 1 litre

- 2 small Napa cabbages (Chinese leaves), about 800g in total
- 20g Maldon salt
- 2 spring onions, trimmed and cut into short lengths
- 50–60g fresh ginger, peeled and roughly chopped (to yield 30g peeled weight)
- 6–7 large garlic cloves, peeled and roughly chopped (again, to yield 30g peeled weight)
- 2 tsp dried red chilli flakes
- 4 large fresh red chillies, de-seeded
- 2 tsp sugar

Slice the cabbage crossways at 4cm intervals and toss with the salt in a very large bowl or stainless steel pan. Just cover with cold water and mix together with your hands to disperse the salt. Leave to soak overnight in the kitchen (this is not the pongy part).

The next day, drain the leaves in a colander, but do not rinse. Return to the wiped-out bowl or pan, add the spring onions and mix together. Put the ginger, garlic, chilli flakes, fresh chillies and sugar into a small food processor and grind to a not-too-fine paste. Add this to the leaves and spring onion and mix together well with a spatula or wooden spoon; you might think hands are best, here, but believe me, they are not (think culinary Lady Macbeth).

Now pack into a preserving jar that will generously accommodate the cabbage and seal. Allow to mature and ferment at room temperature over a period of 4–5 days. Two or three times each day, open the lid to allow gas to escape (the pong), running a chopstick down the inside of the glass to further facilitate this. Although you may think during this period that the mixture smells far too strong, it will mellow and soften, be assured.

Once ready, store the kimchi in the fridge where it will keep for several weeks. I think it is particularly delicious eaten with simply steamed rice, but I can nibble on it at any time. A very healthy food.

Cabbage, caraway & pepper soup with potato dumplings

You may like to further enhance this nourishing soup by sprinkling a little crumbled Roquefort or other good quality, continental blue cheese over each serving.

The recipe for the dumplings will make more than you need. I suggest you keep the extra mixture until the following day, to enjoy the dumplings in their own right – boiled and dressed either with some fonduta (see page 179) or a little hot butter, in which sage leaves have been crisped, and a dusting of freshly grated Parmesan.

Serves 4

for the dumplings

400g potatoes (Desiree are good, here), peeled
40g butter
1 large egg
50g self-raising flour
½ tsp baking powder
1 tsp Maldon salt

for the soup

25g butter
a small glug of olive oil
1 leek, trimmed, well washed and thinly sliced
1 large onion, peeled and finely chopped
1 large carrot, peeled and grated
4 large garlic cloves, peeled and finely chopped
1.25 litres stock
1 tsp caraway seeds
2 tsp freshly ground black pepper, not too fine
salt
300g cabbage (preferably hispi), shredded and then coarsely chopped
1 heaped tbsp chopped parsley

For the dumplings, put the potatoes into a steamer and cook until very tender. Allow them to dry out for a few minutes and, while still hot, pass through a potato ricer (best) or a vegetable mill (mouli-légumes) into a bowl, but try not to over-work them. Now, thoroughly beat in the remaining ingredients and leave to cool and firm up in the fridge.

For the soup, heat the butter and olive oil in another large pan, add the leek, onion, carrot and garlic and fry gently until softened but not coloured. Add the stock, caraway, pepper and salt to taste. Bring up to a simmer and cook for 20 minutes. Meanwhile, bring a large pan of salted water to a gentle boil for the dumplings.

Add the cabbage to the soup and continue to simmer until it is tender. To cook the dumplings, scoop up little balls of potato mixture with an oiled teaspoon and drop them into the boiling water; five per person is about right. They will swell slightly, float up to the surface and be ready in 4–5 minutes.

To assemble, stir the parsley into the simmering soup, decant into four hot soup bowls and add the dumplings. Serve directly.

Chard leaves with wild garlic & olive oil

Wild garlic can be found from around mid-April through May. Keen foragers will know that it grows in deciduous woods and enjoys damp and moist growing conditions, although in the Lake District, where it seems to grow most prolifically, I have picked it from a roadside running along the edge of Ullswater. Otherwise, it may be purchased from a good greengrocer. Wild garlic is also known as Ramsons.

Serves 2

about 250g chard leaves, cut from a 500g bunch (stalks saved for the following recipe), washed
150g wild garlic, washed and thicker stalks removed
2 tbsp olive oil
salt and freshly ground pepper

Slice the chard and wild garlic leaves into wide ribbons. Heat the olive oil in a large frying pan and add the leaves and seasoning. Gently fry, stirring all together well, until beginning to wilt and then allow to stew until soft and tender. About 15–20 minutes all told. Serve piping hot.

Chard gratin

This recipe deals with the stalks, the preceding one uses the equally delicious leaves. They may happily be served as separate dishes, although offering them together could present a most appealing contrast of texture and flavour and make a complete meal for two. Attractive to look at, too, when the cheese-blistered stalks are presented au gratin, alongside a bowl of glossy, dark chard and wild garlic leaves.

Serves 2
30g butter
2 tsp plain flour
225ml milk
30g Gruyère, freshly grated
40g Parmesan, freshly grated
salt, freshly ground white pepper and a scraping of nutmeg
about 250g chard stalks (see above recipe)

Preheat the oven to 200°C/gas mark 6. To make the sauce (Mornay, in fact), melt the butter in a saucepan and stir in the flour. Cook gently for a few minutes, then pour in the milk all in one go and whisk together thoroughly. Place the pan over a low heat and stir constantly until the sauce begins to thicken; any lumps that form will, eventually, disappear (this method has always worked for me).

Add the Gruyère, 25g of the Parmesan and the seasonings. Allow to simmer very gently indeed (a heat-diffuser mat is useful), stirring occasionally, for about 15–20 minutes; this slow cooking makes for a good sauce Mornay – I use it for all Béchamel based sauces.

Meanwhile, peel the chard stalks with a vegetable peeler and cut into 8–10cm lengths. Steam (or boil) until tender, about 20 minutes, then remove and lay on kitchen paper or a tea towel to dry.

Lightly butter a gratin dish and lay the chard stalks in it. Pour over the sauce and sprinkle with the remaining Parmesan. Bake in the oven for about 20 minutes, or until nicely golden and bubbling.

Carrots & Parsnips

When our restaurant Bibendum opened its doors, so pedantically keen was I to do the right thing that we cooked our carottes Vichy in bottles of very expensive Vichy water; well, very expensive is relative, but, when several bottles were being used each day just to cook carrots, the cost began to mount up...

But they were delicious, those carrots, even if their association with Vichy had nothing whatever to do with its mineral water. I guess that the slightly saline, very slightly sweet flavour of Vichy water made them taste so perfectly seasoned. Incidentally, I love to drink Vichy water, too, and it is especially effective when suffering with tummy troubles – it beats 'Dioralyte' any day.

I think certain organic vegetables taste better than others – onions, for instance, some potato varieties and parsnips, too. Big bunches of British blanched winter celery, usually organic, have a particularly wonderful flavour. But, you know, I always see a carrot as, well, just that... a carrot. in this belief. It is what one does to a carrot in the kitchen that makes it taste so much better. Once, friends in Kent (who have a very big garden indeed) presented me with freshly dug parsnips for Sunday lunch. Even their raw scent pervaded the kitchen. The immediacy from earth to table obviously helped hugely, but the intense flavour was just marvellous. Then again, perhaps this was not unusual, as I had never previously eaten freshly dug, home-grown parsnips. Anyway, I simply boiled them and made a purée with much butter and a touch of cream. Jane and Robert still talk of that purée, but you could have boiled them in old bath water and still they would have tasted good, such was their provenance and almost overpowering freshness. One day, of course, they will further shock me with their carrots…

To make a fine purée, it is best to steam the parsnips, cut up into small chunks. Once tender, it is through the finest disk of a mouli-légumes (vegetable mill) that they should, most preferably, be worked. Then it is simply a case of beating in as much butter and cream as seems, at least, sensible, together with salt and plenty of freshly ground white pepper. A spoonful of smooth Dijon mustard whisked in at the very last minute is quite nice, too. Once heated too much, mustard loses its punch so it is better as a late addition.

Kay Henderson's carrot timbal

Kay Henderson, together with her husband, Paul, opened the wonderful Gidleigh Park Hotel on the edge of Dartmoor, Devon, in 1977. This charming little first course was one of the very earliest dishes on the menu when Kay, herself, was in the kitchen. The following recipe is my adaptation to suit this book, but thanks must go to Kay for inspiring the idea in the first place, even though Paul thinks it initially came via the legendary Michel Guèrard.

To give the timbale a pleasing, faintly nubbly texture once cooked, I would recommend first chopping the carrot and onion into small chunks, then pulsing them in a food processor until the texture of coarse sea salt. Together with the melting strands of cheese – and faint aniseed flavour from the chervil – this will produce the most delicate little dish.

Serves 4

50g butter, plus a little extra (softened) for greasing the moulds
400g carrots, peeled and very finely chopped
1 medium onion, about 150g, peeled and very finely chopped
large pinch of sugar
salt and freshly ground pepper
300ml stock
2 large eggs
60g Gruyère or, even better, Beaufort (if you can find it), grated
2 tbsp double cream
2 tbsp finely chopped chervil leaves

for the sauce

1 tbsp sherry vinegar
1 tbsp dry vermouth
25–35g cold butter, cut into small chunks
squeeze of lemon juice (optional)

Preheat the oven to 150°C/gas mark 2. Generously butter four dariole moulds or ramekins and line the base of each with a tiny disc of greaseproof paper.

Using a non-stick frying pan, for preference, melt the butter and quietly fry the carrots and onion with the sugar, a little salt and a generous grinding of pepper until beginning to burnish lightly. Add the stock and allow the mixture to simmer until the carrots are fully cooked and the liquid has reduced by about half.

Place a coarse sieve over a bowl and strain the carrot mixture, stirring it around in the sieve for a moment, but then allowing the liquor to drip through naturally for 10 minutes or so, rather than forcing it. The strained liquid should measure approximately 150ml. Pour it into a small saucepan and set to one side. Tip the carrot pulp into the empty bowl, add the eggs, Gruyère, cream and chervil, and mix well. Check for seasoning.

Pour the carrot mixture into the prepared moulds, filling them to the brim. Cover each with a round of foil and place in a deep baking dish. Pour tap-hot water into the dish until it comes at least three-quarters of the way up the sides of the moulds. Bake in the oven for 20–25 minutes, or until firm to the touch.

To make the sauce, add the vinegar and vermouth to the carrot liquor and reduce it again, by about half. Remove from the heat and whisk in the cold butter, a piece at a time, until the sauce is glossy and richly flavoured. Sharpen with lemon juice only if you wish to.

Once the timbales are cooked, carefully turn out from their ramekins onto warmed plates – not forgetting to remove the little disk of greaseproof paper. Coat with a little of the sauce and serve at once.

Cheese-crusted fried parsnip strips with romesco sauce

Perfect as a wintry Sunday night television supper snack, eaten in front of the fire with fingers and napkins.

The quantities for the romesco will probably make more than you need, but it keeps well in the fridge for several days and is delicious spread onto toasted baguette. Although the ingredients here are mostly from easy bought-in-jars, the end result is very good. I use the Navarrico brand for the piquillo peppers, and Seggiano for the oven-dried tomatoes. If there is enough, use the oil in which the tomatoes have been immersed for the olive oil in the recipe.

Serves 2

350g parsnips, peeled
oil for deep- or shallow-frying (a neutral-flavoured oil, such as sunflower or groundnut)
40g white breadcrumbs made from semi-stale bread
75g Parmesan, freshly grated
¼ tsp cayenne pepper
salt
1 large egg, beaten
flour for coating

for the romesco sauce

40g skinned almonds
4 tbsp olive oil
1 large garlic clove, peeled and chopped
1 small dried chilli
75g oven-dried tomatoes from a jar, drained
75g piquillo peppers from a jar, drained
1 tbsp sherry vinegar
1 tbsp hot water
salt

For the romesco sauce, gently fry the almonds in 1 tsp of the olive oil until golden. Allow to cool, then tip them into a food processor and add the garlic, chilli, tomatoes, peppers, vinegar and hot water. Grind to a nubbly purée and then add salt to taste. Adjust the quantity of vinegar if you wish for a sharper flavour.

Cut the parsnips into finger lengths, about 6cm long, and steam until only just tender, then set aside to cool on a plate.

Mix the breadcrumbs with the cheese, cayenne and salt in a shallow dish. Have the beaten egg ready in a similar dish, and the flour in another one. To coat the parsnips, first dip the strips in flour, then in the egg and, finally, turn them through the breadcrumb/cheese mixture.

To fry the parsnip strips, either use a deep-fat fryer or a deep frying pan containing a 2cm depth of oil. Heat the oil to 170°C in the deep-fryer or, if using the frying pan method, until a small cube of bread turns golden in a minute or so.

Fry the parsnips in the hot oil in batches until crisp and golden, then briefly drain on kitchen paper. Serve at once, with the sauce alongside.

Carrot salad with coriander & green chilli

A nice autumnal dish that is delicious in itself, but also good eaten alongside the new season's garlic, saffron & tomato quiche (on page 88). Fresh, zingy and magnificently inexpensive.

Serves 4

300g carrots, peeled and finely grated
1 ½ tsp Maldon salt
1 ½ tsp caster sugar
juice of 1 small lime
1 tsp coriander seeds
coriander leaves picked from 4–5 bushy sprigs
1 large green chilli, de-seeded

In a large bowl, mix the grated carrot together with the salt, sugar and lime juice. Leave to macerate for at least 30 minutes.

Meanwhile, place the coriander seeds in a small, dry frying pan and gently toast them over a low heat until they smell very good, but be careful not to burn them. Tip into a mortar and lightly crush with the pestle.

Now finely chop the coriander and chilli together (this makes for a more aromatic mix, in a similar way to persillade – garlic and parsley given the same treatment). Add to the carrots together with the coriander seeds and mix well. Turn into a serving dish.

Masala paste

I find this to be a most useful commodity kept at the back of the fridge in a sealed jar (the Le Parfait brand is ideal, here), and further kept in good shape by a film of oil over the surface. When some of the paste is used, simply smooth over the surface and add a tiny bit more oil to cover.

This paste is ever so useful for all sorts of vegetable, pulse and rice preparations when a complex whiff of Asian spice is called for.

4 tbsp cumin seeds
2 tbsp coriander seeds
2 tsp fennel seeds
2 tsp brown mustard seeds
2 tsp whole cloves
2 tsp small, dried red chillies, or a little more if you like it hot
small handful of curry leaves, slightly less, if dried (optional)
300g onions, peeled and chopped
125g garlic cloves, peeled and chopped
150g fresh ginger, peeled and chopped
2 tbsp tamarind paste
2 tsp turmeric
2 tbsp red wine vinegar
100g creamed coconut
2 tsp Maldon salt
2 tsp caster sugar

Using a non-stick frying pan, lightly toast the whole spices: cumin, coriander, fennel and mustard seeds, cloves and chillies, until smelling quite wonderful and pungent, but be careful not to burn them. Tip into a small bowl to cool. Once the spices are cool, process them in a coffee grinder, or similar, until powdered.

Place the curry leaves, onions, garlic, ginger, tamarind paste, turmeric, vinegar, coconut, salt and sugar in a food processor. Add the freshly ground spices and process everything until as smooth as possible; this will depend on the sharpness of your blade and the power of the machine. (Do not be tempted to add the spices whole, as they will remain 'bitty' if not previously powdered.)

There is enough here to fill 2 small Le Parfait jars of 350ml capacity. Cover with a film of oil and store in the fridge until needed.

Parsnip soup with masala cream

This is the time to make a batch of Indian masala paste (see right). Of course, parsnip soup has always had an affinity with curry, for whom I would say, we have the estimable Jane Grigson to thank.

Serves 4
50g butter
1 large leek, trimmed, washed and sliced
500g parsnips, peeled and diced
75ml dry sherry
750ml stock
salt

for the masala cream
200ml double cream
2–3 tsp masala paste, to taste

Melt the butter in a roomy pot and gently sweat the leek until soft.

Add the parsnips and cook, covered, over a very low heat, for a further 5 minutes or so. Remove the lid, turn up the heat and pour in the sherry. Bubble hard for a few minutes until most of the liquid has been driven off, then add the stock. Season with salt to taste and bring up to a low simmer. Cover once more and cook until the parsnips are very soft, about 25 minutes.

Meanwhile, for the masala cream, pour the cream into a small saucepan and whisk in the masala paste. Warm through, cover and leave to infuse.

Once the parsnips are cooked, tip the soup into a blender, process until smooth and then pass through a fine sieve into a clean pan; by the way, I like my creamed soups to be really smooth and silky. Reheat gently, adding a little more stock or water if the soup is too thick.

Ladle into warmed bowls and spoon some of the masala cream on top of each serving, allowing each person to stir it in to flavour the soup.

Peas & Beans

My friend Sarah de Teliga, who is Australian, but has lived off and on in Paris for a number of years, recently related to me a both sweet and sad little histoire regarding a French friend of her son, Linus. They were probably about 10 or 11 years old at the time, Sarah thinks, and Linus had invited his friend home for supper one early summer evening, after school. Sarah had roasted a delicious chicken, perhaps, and accompanied it with some peak of the season haricots verts très fin – in other words, very fine French beans which are the width of pipe cleaners.

All seemed to be going well, although the boy appeared to be a bit shy, Sarah thought. It was not until she noticed a trickle of tears rolling down his increasingly pink cheeks, that she realised there was a more underlying problem than simply shyness: the boy was clearly troubled by something. Sarah discreetly enquired as to what the problem might be by nudging Linus, but was met with a (recently learnt, no doubt) Gallic shrug. Then she asked of the poor boy as to what his dilemma might be, by which time he was convulsed by full-blown blubbing.

Well, it transpired that he had grave concerns over the fact that although Sarah's haricots verts très fin had been 'topped', they had not, at all, been 'tailed'. There followed a clear qualification for his distress, that his Mother would never have countenanced such a lamentable faux pas. Quite simply, the boy was not going to eat them. Sarah then asked him what he would like to do. He said, most emphatically, that he would be going home, now. So, home he went.

Whether the boy was ever invited back for supper and, if he was, had Sarah tried to be more diligent with her beans, I have never enquired. But, much as I adore Sarah, who loves to cook and has a notable affinity with good food (her younger son, Nestor, tells me that Sarah's version of my rice pudding recipe is better than mine), I am with the boy on this one; though, perhaps, with a little more politesse and tantrum-free.

To not tail a French bean (the spiky end) is never considered by French cooks. The very idea is inconceivable. I just hope that what I believe started as a lazy British habit – and first noted by me around about the mid-1980s – does not travel across La Manche. They get stuck in your teeth, those nasty little spikes and, therefore, utterly spoil the pleasure of eating such bundles of sweet tenderness at each and every mouthful. For me, this heretical behaviour is as bad as serving boiled potatoes with their skins remaining attached. Consider yourselves informed.

I wonder how impressed the fastidious French boy would have been with the dish of fresh peas I was once served in the top floor restaurant of the London Hilton: every single pea had been individually peeled!

Now, I know I can often be accused of an (impeccably) mannered approach to certain cookery practices (see above), but even I have never been tempted to peel peas. However, it must here be said that these peas were indeed impeccable and absolutely delicious; so green and tender, and further finished with good butter. Each pea had naturally split in half as dried 'split' peas do. In a similar fashion, so too do broad beans, though here the task is infinitely easier. And, worry not, a recipe does not follow here, where I ask of you to 'Hilton' your peas.

Petit pois à la française

Clearly, the finest peas for this classy and lovely French dish would be ones that you have freshly picked and podded – either home-grown, or collected from a pick-your-own farm. If not, there is little point in using podded peas from, say, a supermarket. Tempting and labour-free though these might seem, they can often be worthless in terms of taste and texture, as any fresh sweetness they may have once had will have turned to starch. If in doubt, I would always suggest frozen – and the more petit, the better. The mint is very un-French, but I like it, here.

Serves 4
100g butter, softened
1 large Cos lettuce
6 spring onions, white part only, thickly sliced
500g frozen peas
salt and freshly ground white pepper
several mint leaves, chopped

Preheat the oven to 160°C/gas mark 3. Bring a pan of salted water to the boil. Take a lidded, shallow ovenproof pan and thickly smear the inside – both bottom and sides – with about one-third of the butter. Separate about 10–12 large, outer dark green leaves from the lettuce (depending on the size of your pan) and briefly blanch in the boiling water until just beginning to flop. Plunge into iced water and lay out to dry on a tea towel.

Carefully and neatly lay the blanched lettuce leaves in the pan, placing the core ends in the middle with the rounded ends of the leaves creeping up the sides, overlapping them slightly and pressing them onto the butter so that they stick. The end result should look like a large, green flower. Reserve a couple of leaves for the top.

Cut the remaining lettuce – the heart – across into shreds and put into a bowl. Add the spring onions, peas, seasoning, mint and a further one-third of the butter, in flecks. Mix together and carefully tip into the lettuce-lined pan. Press down lightly and lay the reserved leaves on top. Now bring the edges of the lining leaves over the top to form a kind of 'lettuce lid'. Melt the remainder of the butter and spoon over the surface.

Cut a greaseproof paper circle slightly bigger than the diameter of the pan, dampen it, and then lightly press down onto the lettuce surface and against the sides of the pan. This 'cartouche' helps to ensure that as much moisture as possible remains within the pea stew as it cooks. There should be no need for any added liquid.

Finally, place the lid on the pan and slide into the oven. Cook for about 1 hour. A good sign that it is ready is when the lettuce and peas have become a dull green colour and are very soft indeed. In fact, for me, the end result should almost be redolent of the best-quality tinned peas!

Fine beans in a cream vinaigrette with shallots

Use the very finest beans you can find, for this one.

Serves 4
500g fine thin French beans, topped and tailed
salt and freshly ground pepper
1 level tbsp good-quality Dijon mustard
1 tbsp white wine or tarragon vinegar
2 shallots, peeled and finely chopped
150ml whipping cream
generous sprinkling of chopped parsley

Add the beans to a pan of fiercely boiling salted water and cook briskly until just tender, but not 'squeaky' to the bite. Drain and refresh in iced water to stop the cooking and set the colour. Drain once more and lay on a clean tea towel to dry thoroughly.

In a bowl, whisk together the mustard, vinegar and some seasoning. Add the shallots and whisk in the cream. Taste the vinaigrette for seasoning.

Arrange the beans in a serving dish, spoon over the dressing and sprinkle generously with chopped parsley to serve.

Marrow fat pea and potato samosas

These samosas do not use traditional Indian pastry, but the filling tastes – to me, at least – authentic and good. You will need both a quantity of green paste and masala paste. However, once these are made, the assembly of the samosas takes very little time, especially as the 'pastry' I have chosen to use is from a packet of oriental spring roll wrappers.

I have also come across frozen packets of samosa pastry in supermarkets, complete with folding instructions on the back of the packet.

It is important to keep the wrappers moist while working with them. Have a damp tea towel to hand to keep the remainder covered as you work with each one.

Makes about 40 small samosas

700g potatoes (preferably Desiree), washed
2 tbsp oil or ghee
1 onion, peeled and finely chopped
1 ½ tbsp masala paste (see page 55)
1 x 300g tin Farrows marrow-fat peas, drained
1 tbsp green paste (see page 157)
salt
juice of ½ lemon
1 heaped tbsp chopped coriander leaves
20 sheets spring roll wrappers, 15cm square
1 large egg, beaten
oil for shallow- or deep-frying

Steam (preferably) or boil the potatoes in their skins until tender. Drain and cool, then peel and cut into chunks. Heat the oil or ghee in a pan and gently fry the onion until golden brown. Add the masala paste and stir around for a minute or two to cook the spices. Remove from the heat, tip in the peas and potatoes and mix well. Now stir in the green paste and a little salt, breaking up the vegetables somewhat at the same time. Sharpen the mixture with lemon juice and mix in the chopped coriander. Tip into a bowl and allow to cool completely.

To form each samosa, cut a wrapper in half, to give two rectangles. Take one of these and place a teaspoonful of the pea and potato mix at one end. Brush the edges with egg and then fold one-third of the rectangle over the filling into a triangle shape. Now fold this one-third over again, but in the opposite direction. Finally, fold this over onto the final one-third to form a completed, triangular package. Squeeze the edges together with your fingers to form a tight seal and move on to the next one. Set the completed samosas aside on a tray or plate; it does not matter one jot, now, if they begin to dry out a little.

To cook the samosas, heat a 2–3 cm depth of oil in a frying pan (or use a deep-fryer) over a medium heat until it reaches 170°C. To check the oil is hot enough, drop in a cube of bread; it should turn golden within a minute or so. Fry 4 or 5 samosas at a time, being careful not to overcrowd the pan. Fry gently, turning the samosas frequently until they are crisp and golden. (I sometimes transfer them to a flat tray in a medium oven, to both keep hot and become more golden and crisp, turning them occasionally.) Drain on kitchen paper and serve hot.

A good, instant dip can be made by mixing plain yoghurt with lots of chopped mint, a little chopped green chilli, a pinch of sugar and salt, and a squeeze of lime juice. I also find some mango chutney is a further, essential condiment.

A small stew of broad beans with summer savory

Summer savory has always been seen as a fine partner to broad beans. Although not a herb readily available in the supermarkets, it may be found in pots at garden centres or, of course, you could grow your own from seed. Lemon thyme and tarragon are other possibilities for this stew.

Serves 2

2kg broad beans, podded
40g butter
1 small onion (preferably white), peeled and finely chopped
salt and freshly ground white pepper
200ml whipping cream
2 tsp chopped summer savory leaves
squeeze of lemon juice

Add the broad beans to a pan of boiling salted water and boil for 2–3 minutes only. Drain.

Melt the butter in a pan, add the onion and stew for a few moments until softened. Now tip in the beans and turn them around in the buttery onions for a few seconds, then pour in the cream. Bring up to the boil and simmer until the liquor has thickened and the beans are tender.

Stir in the savory and lemon juice and serve without delay. Very delicious spooned over a slice of bruschetta.

Leeks & Onions

There was a time when the lovely leek was simply not available for purchase during the summer months. Or, if there were some late spring stragglers, their centres – often making up about two-thirds of the vegetable – would be nothing but impenetrable woody sticks. Not so now, with perfect leeks being available all year round in supermarkets – and in perfect condition.

I do not necessarily agree with all out-of-season imports; Peruvian asparagus appearing on the shelves when Surrey spears that I cut myself have been available for at least 2 weeks, is one particular irritation. However, I must admit, the leek situation suits me down to the ground, as it allows me to enjoy my most favourite cold leek and potato soup, the dreamily delicious vichyssoise, all summer long.

I adore this pale, pale soup, just with the merest hint of background green to its cool and creamy appearance. In fact, I have often wondered whether there has ever been a house paint named after vichyssoise, so pretty would it look in a bathroom or sunny kitchen. Anyway, interior design aside, another important aspect of the soup should be that of limpid and not at all thick. It should pour easily when served and be almost as thin as the consistency of whipping cream, which, I would suggest is the cream to employ when making vichyssoise, rather than an overly rich double cream.

Like all cold soups, vichyssoise should be thoroughly chilled for maximum enjoyment, otherwise they are neither one thing nor the other. I have often debated with fellow cooks as to whether one should use butter when stewing the leeks at the initial stages of making vichyssoise. After all, once chilled, the butter content, however well homogenised in the blending thereof, will remain as minute, chilled butter flecks. I have tried using no fats whatsoever, simply simmering the leeks and potatoes together in well seasoned stock, before blending in the cream, but I don't think it has quite enough flavour and has a bit of a 'boiled' taste to it.

I now admit to having had the best success with one of those 'spreadable butters' (awful name, I know), which are made by blending butter with a neutral oil. Once the sliced leeks – and almost all white parts, please – have cooked to a semi-soft consistency, add roughly the same quantity of small pieces of chopped, peeled potatoes (a variety that you can trust to break up easily) and stew both vegetables together until softened. Cover generously with half stock and half milk, simmer until the potatoes are collapsing and then liquidise until super-smooth. Pass through a fine sieve, stir in some whipping cream and chill. Serve in ice-cold soup bowls and scatter generously with snipped chives.

Onions – which haven't had as much of a look-in, here – are equally delicious when given the same treatment, but as a hot soup. So, butter is fine now, and good stock, but without other dairy additions. Finely chopped parsley is the herb to stir in at the end, together with plenty of freshly ground white pepper.

Onion & blood orange salad with olive oil

Does not this recipe qualify as one of the most simple and delicious in this book? – well, delicious in anyone's book, come to that. The secret, of course, is its simplicity, together with the sheer beauty of the thing, once carefully assembled.

And I do urge you to make the most of your knife skills when slicing both oranges and onions: do as thin as you dare! Also, this is one moment in one's culinary life where extra cash should be expended on the extra virgin oil.

Some recipes I have come across for this Sicilian speciality ask that black olives be included in the dish. Traditional it may be, but I urge you to resist. Also, I prefer sweet white onions as opposed to the possibly more usual red ones. Pace!

Serves 2

4 blood oranges
1 or 2 small, sweet white onions, peeled
extra virgin olive oil
freshly ground black pepper

Cut the tops and bottoms off the oranges and, using a small, very sharp knife, further slice off the skins of the oranges cutting close to the flesh and removing all traces of pith. Slice thinly (removing any pips) and arrange neatly, slightly overlapping, on a beautiful plate.

Thinly slice the onions and lay on top of the oranges. Spoon enough olive oil onto the assembly to suit you, and then grind over some pepper. Eat all on its own, and with someone you like very much.

Oriental leeks 'vinaigrette' with salted duck egg

Salted duck eggs are available from Oriental supermarkets and, in my opinion, are quite delicious. Do not, however, confuse them with 'thousand year old eggs', which are an acquired taste to be sure. Simply hard-boil some fresh duck eggs if salted ones are unavailable.

Serves 2

4 medium leeks, trimmed of almost all green parts, or 8 smaller ones
1 garlic clove, crushed and very finely chopped

for the vinaigrette
2 tbsp light soy sauce
1 tbsp sesame oil
1–2 tbsp sunflower oil, or other neutral oil
2 tsp hoisin or plum sauce
1 tbsp lemon juice

to garnish
1 salted (or freshly hard-boiled) duck egg, grated
a little sliced green chilli (optional)
1 tsp very finely sliced spring onion tops
several coriander leaves

If using medium leeks, slice them into 2.5cm lengths; if using small ones, leave them whole. Either way, wash the leeks very thoroughly.

To make the dressing, simply whisk the ingredients together in a small bowl until well amalgamated. Leave to infuse.

Boil the leeks in lightly salted water until tender (or steam them if you like). Lift them out carefully with a slotted spoon and put to drain and cool on a tea-towel.

Arrange the cooled leeks in a suitable dish and spoon over the dressing. Sprinkle over the egg and chilli (if using), together with the spring onion and coriander. Eat as is, or with some plain boiled rice.

Leek & cheese pie

This recipe is based on a cheese and onion pie made by my mother and particularly adored by my brother and I when we were growing up.

Serves 4

for the pastry
125g butter
200g self-raising flour
pinch of salt
ice-cold water, to mix

for the filling
25g butter
3 large leeks, white part only, thinly sliced
1 teacupful of water
salt and freshly ground white pepper
250–300g mature Cheddar, Lancashire or Caerphilly, grated
a little milk, to both seal and glaze the pastry

To make the pastry, cut the butter into small chunks and place in a large bowl with the flour and salt. Gently rub the fat into the flour using fingertips until the texture resembles very coarse breadcrumbs. Mix in enough water to just bind the mixture together as a dough without it becoming too slack and wet; in other words, be cautious with the water. Knead the dough until fully amalgamated, dust with flour and slip into a plastic bag. Place in the fridge to rest for 30 minutes before using.

Preheat the oven to 180°C/gas mark 4 and also place a flat baking sheet in there too, which will help to cook the base of the pie more evenly.

Meanwhile, prepare the filling. Melt the butter in a roomy pan, add the leeks and allow to quietly wilt and stew for 10 minutes over a gentle heat without colouring. Now tip in the water, salt and plenty of pepper. Continue to cook over a similar heat, stirring occasionally, until almost all liquid has been driven off. Decant the leeks onto a plate, spread them out and allow to cool.

Lightly butter a 20cm loose-bottomed tart tin, 4cm deep. On a lightly floured surface, roll out two-thirds of the pastry moderately thinly and use to line the tin. Now roll out the remainder to a round of similar thickness, large enough to use as a lid to the pie. Cover the base of the pie with half of the cooked leeks and then cover with half the grated cheese. Repeat these layers.

Brush the edges of the pastry case with milk. Position the pastry lid and press the edges together lightly to seal, then trim off any excess overhang. Brush the surface of the pie with milk. Make three small incisions in the middle of the pie using the point of a sharp knife and, if you wish, decorate the edge with light indentations from the tines of a fork.

Place the tin on the hot baking sheet and bake the pie on the middle shelf of the oven for about 40–50 minutes, or until pale golden and tiny oozes of cheesy-leeky juices are bubbling up through the holes in the middle of the pie. Remove from the oven and leave for 20 minutes before un-moulding and cutting into generous wedges. Best served warm and extremely good with piccalilli, too.

Boiled onions with poached egg & Lancashire cheese

I was first informed of this quite astonishingly simple bowl of goodness by a young chef who had previously worked at a well renowned Lancashire pub, The Three Fishes, in the village of Mitton. Although 'boiled onions' hardly sounds enticing, it is, in fact, absolutely everything it says – and why on earth call it anything else? 'Fancy names mean nowt', my grandfather would have said, and he was a Lancashire man, too, through and through.

It is imperative to use both white-skinned onions and ground white pepper here, to ensure the correct texture and traditional flavour. I have added a bay leaf, too, which is not in the original recipe; you might prefer to omit it.

Serves 4

- 500g white-skinned onions, peeled and coarsely but neatly diced
- 350ml water
- 50g butter
- scant ½ tsp ready ground white pepper
- 2 tsp Maldon salt
- 1 bay leaf (optional)
- splash of malt vinegar (optional)
- 250–300g Lancashire or similar tasty cheese, coarsely grated
- 4 large eggs
- 2 tbsp finely chopped curly parsley

Put the onions into a pan with the water, butter, pepper, salt and bay leaf, if using. Bring to the boil, turn down to a low simmer, cover and cook for about 30 minutes, or until the onions are nice and soft. Heat the grill to medium. Have ready a pan of simmering water with a healthy splash of malt vinegar added, if desired, to poach the eggs.

Once ready, stir the onions well and then divide between four warmed, ovenproof, shallow dishes. Now sprinkle with the cheese and place under the grill to only just melt the cheese, not to brown it. Meanwhile, poach the eggs in the simmering water. Remove with a slotted spoon to drain and place one on top of each dish of onions and cheese. Sprinkle over the parsley and serve without delay.

Fennel & Celery

It was with enormous pleasure that, on two occasions, I was privileged to lunch at the table of Lulu Peyraud, at Domaine Tempier in Bandol, in the South of France. Her late husband, Lucien, a renowned wine maker of great style, was still alive at the time, producing unique bottles of rare finesse and class with the help of his family. The Tempier rosé remains one of my most favourite summer glasses, with the single vineyard red wines capable of greatness and longevity.

I was taken there by Richard Olney, with our mutual friend, Jill Norman, in the late 1990s. Richard had been a fond friend of the Peyraud family for years. He loved and admired the Domaine's wine but, almost more importantly still, he adored Lulu Peyraud's wonderful cooking. I would almost go as far as to say that he may have perceived Lulu's expertise as second to none. Considering Richard's own substantial talent for cookery and wine writing has no peer, in my view, this can only be seen as praise indeed.

Watching this diminutive woman go about preparing lunch was an absolute joy. Everything was clearly happening a great deal in her kitchen on those few days, yet none of it seemed much in evidence. Quite simply, delicious food appeared at table and we ate it. No ceremony, it was just lunch as normal at the Domaine, eaten out of doors under the shade of vine trellises. Tempier rosé was poured, naturally, and olives and thick slices of saucisson sec were passed around.

Richard was requested to open the difficult, indigenous 'violet' clams, resembling small lumps of craggy rock, with a sharp, stubby oyster knife. When prised apart, they revealed orange flesh of a unique savour. These were our first course. Simply roasted chicken accompanied by yellow and waxy potatoes cooked in the belly of a bulbous, terracotta pot with copious amounts of deep-green Provençal olive oil followed. Whole cloves of garlic, which had softened to an unctuous fondancy, pungently seasoned the dish. 'Best potatoes I can remember', I think I said at the time.

But it was to be the braised fennel served at the second lunch – with a couple of enormous baked bream – that really blew my socks off. Again, it was olive oil and garlic which, respectively, were the chosen emollient and aromatic nuance. A splash of white wine provided lubrication. During the fennel's slow braise, the wine gently emulsified with the oil, producing a lotion of perfection. And, as

I pondered at the time, these were treats eaten every single day, in that perfect place.

Asking of Lulu quite how she had put the fennel together, she typically delivered something along the lines of this:

'Well, you know, just quarter the fennel, colour it a little in plenty of olive oil, put in some sliced garlic, add wine while the pot is hot, season, put on the lid and cook it in the oven until soft and very tender.' Would that all recipes were so eloquently put…

Celery hearts can be prepared in a similar way to Lulu Peyraud's dish above, or you could follow the recipe on page 71, which utilises an intensely flavoured porcini juice. In all cases with celery – and whether eaten raw or cooked – I would always advise peeling the outer stalks of hearts and, when using the larger outside stalks, peel all of them.

Cream of fennel soup with garlic butter

Note that the recipe for the garlic butter will give you much more than you need for the soup. Apart from the impracticality of making a small amount, garlic butter keeps in the freezer very well and is useful to have around – delicious, instant garlic bread or with mushrooms, for instance.

Serves 4

2 tbsp olive oil
2 small onions, peeled and chopped
350g fennel bulb, trimmed and chopped
1 tsp fennel seeds
1 medium potato, peeled and chopped
750ml stock
salt and freshly ground white pepper
150ml whipping cream

for the garlic butter

250g butter, softened
25g garlic, peeled and finely chopped
40g parsley leaves, finely chopped
2 tsp Pernod
¾ tsp salt
¼ tsp black pepper
good pinch of cayenne pepper
3–4 drops Tabasco

Heat the olive oil in a roomy pan, add the onions and gently cook for 20 minutes or so until soft, but not coloured. Add the chopped fennel with the seeds, cover and allow to gently stew for 10 minutes. Add the potato and pour in the stock. Season and bring to a simmer. Cover and cook for 30 minutes, or until the vegetables are almost falling apart.

Meanwhile, to make the garlic butter, simply mix everything together in a bowl, place on a sheet of greaseproof paper and roll up into a kind of Christmas cracker. Wrap in foil to secure the package and put into the freezer to firm up.

Purée the soup well in a blender, then push through a fine sieve into a clean pan. Add the cream and gently reheat. Pour into hot soup bowls and pop a slice of garlic butter onto the surface of each, to melt in.

Fennel salad with lemon & olive oil

A restaurant kitchen has the distinct advantage of a heavy duty deli slicer for cutting fennel into the wispiest of wafer-thin shavings. In a domestic kitchen, one of those razor-sharp Japanese mandolin hand-slicers is the best option. Cut the fennel into quarters before slicing, to fit the width of the blade.

Serves 4

4 small, very fresh bulbs of fennel, trimmed, reserving a few fronds if attached
Maldon salt and freshly ground pepper
juice of 1 lemon
2 tsp Pernod
4 tbsp extra virgin olive oil

Thinly slice the fennel and lay out in a large shallow dish so that it is almost in a single layer. Season and sprinkle over the lemon juice and Pernod. Leave to macerate in a cool place for about 1 hour.

Stir together briefly and once more lay out the slices of fennel; they will now have softened up somewhat. Spoon the olive oil evenly over the fennel. Chop up any reserved feathery fronds and sprinkle over the surface to serve.

Braised fennel & celeriac with Pastis

I know that the interloper celeriac, here, is not strictly 'celery'. However, they are of the same family and, braised together with fennel, it produces a dish of rare subtlety with deliciously fondant textures.

Serves 4
2 fennel bulbs, trimmed
1 medium celeriac
2–3 tbsp olive oil
salt and freshly ground pepper
50g butter
2–3 tbsp Pastis (preferably Ricard)
100ml white wine
juice of 1 small lemon
2 tbsp chopped parsley

Preheat the oven to 150°C/gas mark 2. Cut the fennel lengthways into 8 wedges. Peel the celeriac and cut into fat 'chip' shapes. Heat the olive oil in a lidded, ovenproof cooking pot. Add the fennel and celeriac, season and gently turn them in the oil until lightly gilded, about 15 minutes or so.

Add the butter and allow to froth, then turn down the heat. Season and add the Pastis and wine. Spoon these juices over the vegetables, add the lemon juice and allow to bubble gently. Now cover and bake in the oven for about 1 hour, until really soft and meltingly tender. Stir in the chopped parsley and serve directly from the pot.

Celery hearts in mushroom juice, vermouth & tarragon

One of my late Father's Christmas contributions was to always braise some celery to accompany the turkey. I never knew exactly what he did to it, but this is my version, in memoriam.

Serves 4
20g dried porcini mushrooms
200ml hot stock
50g butter
4 celery hearts, outer stalks peeled
1 tbsp tarragon vinegar
1 small garlic clove, bruised
50ml vermouth (fragrant Noilly Prat is ideal)
1 tbsp chopped tarragon, plus a little extra for garnish
pinch of celery salt
freshly ground white pepper

Preheat the oven to 180°C/gas mark 4. Put the dried porcini in a bowl, pour on the stock and leave to soak for 15 minutes. Melt the butter in an ovenproof cast-iron dish. Add the celery and gently stew until lightly coloured, then add the vinegar. Allow to bubble and reduce to almost nothing before adding the porcini and stock. Bring to the boil and slip in the garlic, together with the vermouth, tarragon, celery salt and pepper.

Cover with foil and braise in the oven for 40 minutes to 1 hour, turning the celery over halfway through. Check from time to time that there is enough liquid, lowering the temperature and adding a little more stock

if things start to look to dry.

To serve, lift out the deliciously limp celery, place it on a hot serving dish, strain the juices over and sprinkle with the extra tarragon. Surprisingly good draped over a serving of nicely old-fashioned creamed potatoes.

Curry 'essence'

This curry essence from Constance Spry's Coronation chicken recipe is the one I have always used. For me, it is correct and authentic. You won't need all of it for the salad, but it will keep in a screw-top jar in the fridge for 3–4 weeks. It is also used in oeufs 'mollet' à l'indiènne (see page 191).

Serves 4

1 tbsp sunflower oil
50g chopped onion
2 tsp good quality Madras curry powder
1 heaped tsp tomato purée
150ml red wine
120ml water
1 bay leaf
salt, sugar, a touch of pepper
juice of ½ lemon
2 tbsp apricot jam or mango chutney

Heat the oil in a pan and gently stew the onion until transparent. Add the curry powder and cook for a few minutes longer. Stir in the tomato purée and cook for a few moments, then add all the other ingredients. Bring to a simmer and cook for a further 10–15 minutes. Strain through a fine sieve, pressing it through with a small ladle. Allow to cool.

Crisp celery & apple salad in curry cream dressing

To fashion the curry cream sauce for this, you will first need to make the curry 'essence' (opposite), as I like to refer to it.

Serves 2

2 Granny Smith apples, peeled
4 crisp celery sticks, peeled
1 tbsp sultanas, plumped
for 10 minutes in a little boiling water
generous squeeze of lemon juice
150ml double cream
2–3 tbsp curry essence, or to taste (see opposite)
cayenne pepper

Cut the apples and celery into thick matchsticks. Carefully mix together with the sultanas and lemon juice in a roomy bowl. Chill thoroughly for 30 minutes.

In another smaller bowl, beat together the cream and curry essence until loosely thickened. Fold into the apple and celery, turn into a serving dish and sprinkle lightly with cayenne.

A perfect light lunch eaten out of doors – and relatively healthy. So promptly ruin that with a nice cold beer or two.

Lettuce & Cucumber

My friend Rowley Leigh,serves a perfect green salad. He calls it 'lettuce heart salad' and that is exactly what it is: carefully rinsed and dried, pale yellow leaves taken from what we know as a round lettuce, slightly separated and then each one dressed with just the correct amount of a judicious vinaigrette – and nothing else at all!

Some might say that if a salad is green, it may include such items as sliced cucumber and green pepper, or watercress and rocket. Well, I absolutely loathe any such thing, but the maker would be right: the items listed are all green, after all. However, a green salad, for me, will always be that which Rowley does so beautifully. So much, in fact, do I enjoy this salad, that it makes a perfect first course all on its own, even though there is a huge offering of other delicacies upon which to feast.

The round lettuce is a delicious, simply flavoured variety and one which will be almost unknown, these days, to the munchers of pre-packed mixed leaves, so easy to just tip into a bowl and add a splash of dressing from a bottle. Okay, I am no snob, but in late spring and the summer months, when the home-grown round lettuce comes into its own, there seems little excuse not to quickly wash and spin the hearts of this fresh little lettuce, rather than to rely upon the easy route of the ubiquitous bag.

And to talk further of simple salads, the cucumber comes into its own when treated in this way. As far as I know, they still serve an impeccable salade de concombres at the legendary, old Parisian bistrot, Allard – a bistro de-luxe, some might say, which boasted two Michelin stars when Madame Allard was at the stove long ago. The cucumber is peeled, naturally, cut in half lengthways and its seeds removed, then thinly sliced into half-moons. It is then salted and left to disgorge its juices for a couple of hours or so. Once squeezed dry in a tea towel, it is dressed with a light mustard vinaigrette made with salad oil, not olive oil, and served sprinkled with a little finely chopped chervil or parsley. Here, once again, the salad is only offered on the menu during the summer.

Some say that Caesar Cardini, the creator of Caesar Salad did not, in fact, include anchovies in his impromptu original. Well, be that as it may... Naturally, there are none in the following recipe either. And, furthermore, depending on how strict a vegetarian one is, the use of Worcestershire sauce should also be avoided, including, as it surely does, anchovies in its maceration process.

However, you will be thrilled to know that for those wishing to be absolutely strict, I have devised a nifty alternative using mushroom ketchup: simply mix 1 tsp Tabasco and 1 heaped tsp caster sugar into 75ml of mushroom ketchup and shake to dissolve the sugar. If wishing to compare, you will be pleasantly surprised by the similarity. Double or triple the quantities and make up a larger batch for frequent use, if you like. Naturally, it keeps for ages.

Caesar salad

A sourdough baguette is very good for making the croûtons, here. Please resist the urge to 'shave' the Parmesan, which misses the point of the dish, as the cheese really needs to become part of the dressing.

Serves 4

30g butter
2 tbsp olive oil
2 garlic cloves, peeled and crushed
100g good bread, cubed
salt and freshly ground pepper
2 large eggs
3–4 crisp Cos lettuce hearts
40g Parmesan, freshly grated

for the dressing

3 garlic cloves, peeled and crushed with ½ tsp salt, to a paste
2 tsp lemon juice
2–3 tsp Worcestershire sauce, or my alternative (see page 76)
pepper
125ml extra virgin olive oil

Preheat the oven to 180°C/gas mark 4. In a small pan, warm the butter and olive oil gently with the garlic and allow to infuse for 5 minutes, or so. Strain the oily butter into a bowl. Add the bread, season and toss with your hands, then lift out onto kitchen paper. Scatter the bread cubes on a baking tray and bake for about 10 minutes until crisp and golden.

Add the eggs to a pan of boiling water and boil for 2 minutes, then immediately drain and cool them under cold running water. Now crack each one open and scoop out the runny egg into a bowl. Break up with a fork until it is sloppy.

To make the dressing, in the bowl in which you will serve the salad, mix the garlic with the lemon juice, Worcestershire sauce and plenty of pepper. Whisk in the olive oil until emulsified.

Separate the lettuce leaves and wash in very cold water, then spin or shake dry. Now briefly toss the croûtons in the dressing so they absorb a little of it, and then add the lettuce and sloppy eggs. Lightly toss together and sprinkle with Parmesan to serve.

English lettuce salad with tarragon cream dressing

The above dressing originates from one of my old Cordon Bleu magazines, where it is used to dress pears, as a sweet-savoury first course. An unusual pairing (sorry), one might think, but strangely delicious.

Serves 6

- 4–5 round lettuces, trimmed of all floppy, outer greenery
- ½ cucumber, peeled and sliced
- 6 spring onions, trimmed and sliced into short lengths
- 1 bunch of radishes, trimmed, washed and quartered
- 4 boiled eggs, peeled and quartered or sliced
- 1–2 bunches of watercress, depending on size, washed and dried

for the dressing

- 2 large eggs
- 2 tsp caster sugar
- 3 tbsp tarragon vinegar
- pinch of salt
- 250ml whipping cream
- 1 tbsp chopped tarragon
- a little milk (optional)

First make the dressing. Put the eggs, sugar, vinegar and salt in the top of a double boiler, or in a glass bowl suspended over a pan of barely simmering water and beat together, using an electric hand whisk for the speediest result. Continue until the mixture is thick and mousse-like; the beaters should leave a thick trail when the whisk is lifted. Remove from the heat and continue beating until lukewarm. Cool.

Loosely whip the cream and fold into the dressing, together with the chopped tarragon; if you feel the dressing is a touch too thick, thin with a little milk.

For the salad, separate the lettuce leaves and carefully wash in very cold water, then spin or shake dry and lay out onto a handsome, large platter. Attractively arrange the cucumber, spring onions, radishes and eggs over the leaves. Pick the watercress into small sprigs and strew over the salad. Spoon over the dressing and serve at once.

Cucumber, melon & tomato salad

Having learnt to cook through the 1970s, I have a soft spot for the funny old melon-baller. If you don't have one, or have no intention of owning such a thing, then cut the melon into 8 boat shapes, remove the flesh with a sharp knife and cut into small wedges.

Serves 4

200g small, ripe tomatoes, cored
1 cucumber, about 300g, peeled
1 Charentais melon, about 500g, cut in half and de-seeded
salt and freshly ground pepper
4 tsp raspberry vinegar
80ml extra virgin olive oil
2 tsp snipped chives
1 tbsp shredded mint

Put the tomatoes into a bowl, pour on boiling water and count to ten, then drain. Peel the tomatoes, cut them in half and place in a bowl.

Cut the cucumber in half and then slice each piece lengthways in two. Scoop the seeds out, using a teaspoon (or melon baller), then slice the 4 lengths into thick-ish slices with a slight diagonal bias, simply for a more pleasing look. Add to the tomatoes.

Make balls or wedges from the melon and add to the tomatoes and cucumber. Season lightly and add the remaining ingredients. Toss gently and leave in the fridge to macerate for at least 30 minutes before serving.

Eat with toasted slices of baguette, delicately rubbed with a cut garlic clove and brushed with olive oil.

Buttered cucumber with mustard cress & mint

This simple, summery and fragrant little dish is very pleasing eaten warm with slices of thinly buttered rye bread, spread with curd or cream cheese – or with goat's curd, which is especially delicious.

Serves 2

1 cucumber, peeled
25g butter, plus a little extra to finish
salt and freshly ground pepper
small pinch of sugar
2 punnets of mustard cress
1 tbsp chopped mint
1–2 tsp white wine vinegar

Cut the cucumber in half and then slice each piece lengthways in two. Cut the 4 lengths into thick-ish slices, with a slight diagonal bias. Melt the butter in a deep frying pan and add the cucumber. Season, add the sugar and allow to gently stew for a few minutes until softened but not soggy.

Now, using a pair of scissors, snip the cress all over the surface and strew with the mint. Turn up the heat, toss the cucumber around with a wooden spoon and mix well. Finally, add the vinegar and a touch more butter just to add a final gloss. Turn into a shallow dish and serve warm.

Garlic & Shallots

As it seeps out of early morning metropolitan restaurant kitchen vents when office-bound folk are on their way to their desks in giant, equality open-plan rooms stacked one on top of the other, the aroma of chopped garlic and shallots stewing together in butter defies eloquent description. As they pass by the busy commis chef's first shift in his hot basement, these striding, be-suited types, might mutter thus: 'Mmmm...' or 'Ahhhh... that smells soooo good!'

These two intimate alliums begin so many savoury stews and braises that it is difficult to imagine such dishes without this familiar overture. Moreover, not to marry them seems inconceivable to the home cook who enjoys being in their kitchen, making family meals with pleasure, day in, day out. Admittedly a rare thing, these days, but such folk do still exist.

Indian vegetarian cookery, to generalise, is a case in point – for the onion/garlic pairing, as well as the regular making of family meals. Ghee, rather than butter, would be the grease of choice here, so that a higher temperature may be achieved, as cooks of that country prefer to take the cooking of both onion and garlic almost to a point of no return. And I have always believed that this is where us amateurs of curry-making – to use a prosaic description – fall short: we simply dare not deeply burnish, and therefore our attempts often fall short of authenticity.

I recall a stew of aubergine that I once ate in a simple formica-topped table establishment in Southall, very west London (almost adjacent to Heathrow airport's runway), together with an Australian friend who adored Indian food but who was bereft of such delights in Sydney. It was an exact example of the benefit given to the bland aubergine by deep golden shreds of onions and garlic.

The slippery-sloppy fingers of that naturally spongy vegetable had, you see, soaked up all those toasted flavours, so taking it onto quite another plane. Yes, there was also finely minced fresh ginger root and cumin seed in there too, as well as lots of chopped coriander leaf and green chilli, but the basis of this wonderfully oily dish relied, most heavily, upon that richly golden onion and garlic.

There is much discussion as to whether the wispy, often acrid green germ within a garlic clove should be removed prior to cooking; I am quite convinced that the Asian restaurant cook would not bother to so do. A great deal of garlic, after all, is prepared daily in all such kitchens and, what with the chore of peeling hundreds of cloves as it is, the very idea of splitting each one in half and winkling out said green germ would be anathema to the poor kitchen lad.

Personally, I would recommend removing the germ if preparing more subtle European dishes, particularly if using raw, and especially if the garlic seems a little less than sprightly; if the cloves are at all dry and leathery, then they should be discarded anyway, and fresher garlic sourced at once.

However, I have discovered it is often best to find big fat heads of fresh, new season's garlic in the spring, purchase in plenty, store carefully and keep a check on how they are faring over time. I have been pleasantly surprised to discover that the germ is rarely, if ever, revealed by the time of exhaustion.

New season's garlic, saffron & tomato quiche

It should be noted that the quiche filling will be far too strong if it is made with anything other than fresh, new season's garlic cloves, however many times they have been blanched in boiling water.

Serves 4

for the pastry
100g plain flour
65g butter, cut into cubes
pinch of salt
1–2 tbsp iced water

for the filling
100g peeled new season's garlic cloves
salt and freshly ground pepper
200g ripe tomatoes, peeled and chopped
100ml milk
1 tsp saffron threads
2 large eggs
1 large egg yolk
100ml soured cream
100ml double cream
100g light cream cheese
30g Parmesan, freshly grated

For the pastry, put the flour, butter and salt into a food processor and briefly blend together until the mixture resembles fine breadcrumbs. Now tip into a large, roomy bowl and gently mix in the water, using cool hands or a knife, until well amalgamated. Knead together, then put into a plastic bag and rest in the fridge for at least 1 hour before rolling.

For the filling, put the garlic cloves into a small pan, cover with water and bring to the boil. Drain and refresh with cold water, then repeat. Drain and refresh again, cover with water once more, add a little salt and simmer for several minutes until very soft. Drain and set aside.

Put the tomatoes and a little seasoning into a stainless steel pan and allow to simmer for a good half an hour or so, at least until the mixture is well reduced and jammy (it needs to be spread onto the pastry base).

Preheat the oven to 180°C/gas mark 4 and put a baking sheet inside to heat up. Roll out the pastry on a lightly floured surface as thinly as you dare, then use to line a 20cm tart tin, 3cm deep and prick the base. Line the pastry case with foil and dried beans, slide onto the hot baking sheet and bake 'blind' for about 15 minutes. Remove the foil and beans and return the pastry case to the oven for a further 10–15 minutes until it is golden, crisp and well cooked through, particularly the base.

Put the milk into a small pan with the saffron, warm through and leave to infuse for 5 minutes. Whiz the eggs, egg yolk and cooked garlic together in a food processor until smooth. Add both creams, the cream cheese and

Parmesan and briefly blend again. Pour into a bowl and stir in the saffron-infused milk. Season lightly.

To assemble the tart, spread the tomato over the pastry base and then pour in the saffron custard; you may find it less nerve-racking to half-fill the case first and spoon or ladle in the rest once it is in the oven. Bake for 30–40 minutes until set and pale golden on the surface. Allow to cool for at least 10 minutes before eating, as hot quiche tastes of very little.

Fresh garlic purée

This purée is very good with grilled aubergines and courgettes, or with halved fennel bulbs that have been par-boiled and then oven-roasted.

It is also delicious spread onto bruschetta and topped with sliced tomatoes or hard-boiled eggs, or both.

Makes about 350–400ml
3 large heads of new season's garlic
salt and freshly ground white pepper
250g crème fraîche

Separate and peel the garlic cloves, then simmer in salted water until just tender; drain. Purée the garlic in a food processor, but leave a little grainy. Tip into a bowl and allow to cool completely. Add the crème fraîche and beat with a whisk until thick. Add more salt to taste and grind in plenty of white pepper.

Crisp fried shallots.

These shards of deeply savoury onion-y-ness are wonderful when tossed into all kinds of salads. They are also good sprinkled over a Welsh rarebit, or a cream of onion or leek and potato soup in place of the more traditional croûtons. Slices of garlic can be given a similar treatment, but these should not be taken as far as the shallots – more of a pale golden – as they can become horribly burnt and bitter.

6–8 shallots, or more
oil for frying (a neutral-flavoured oil, such as sunflower or groundnut)
Maldon salt

Peel and thickly slice the shallots – to about twice the thickness of a £1 coin. Put them into a deep frying pan, just cover with oil and place over a medium heat. When the shallots begin to sizzle, start to stir them around with a kitchen fork, gently separating them as they cook. Keeping the heat moderate, continue to fry until they have turned a rich, golden brown and are deeply frazzled; lift one or two out and check for crispness, although they will crisp up even more, once drained. Lift out the shallots using a slotted spoon, drain on a double layer of kitchen paper and sprinkle with fine sea salt.

Sweet & sour shallots

These would be good eaten with a piping hot cauliflower cheese (see page 32) or macaroni cheese with tomatoes (see page 161). As the amount of shallots here is quite a handful – well, much more than that – it is worth pouring some boiling water over them before peeling, as this eases the task. Leave in the water for a couple of minutes, then drain.

Serves 4–6

500g small shallots, peeled
120ml sherry vinegar
200ml water
100ml olive oil
1 ½ tbsp tomato purée
40g sugar
salt and freshly ground pepper
2 bay leaves
2 rosemary sprigs
50g currants
chopped parsley to garnish

Preheat the oven to 140°C/gas mark 1. Put the shallots into a lidded, solid cooking pot. Whisk together the vinegar, water, olive oil, tomato purée and sugar, then add salt and pepper to taste. Pour over the shallots and add the bay leaves and rosemary. Now stir in the currants, while also making sure that the shallots are submerged in the liquids.

Bring to a simmer on top of the stove and gently cook for a few minutes, stirring a little to mingle the ingredients together. Once gently bubbling, put on the lid and slide into the oven. Cook for about 1 hour 20 minutes, until the shallots are soft, but not falling apart. I suggest that you check after 1 hour, just to be sure. Serve at room temperature, sprinkled with chopped parsley.

Ginger & Spring Onions

It is the Chinese we must thank for the burst of flavour given by the pairing of shredded ginger and spring onions. When added to various dishes from that country, they work in a similar way to golden fried onions and garlic, which combine to enhance stews, braises and, particularly, curries. With ginger and spring onions, it is most often in their raw state, or added during the last moments of cooking, where these aromatic flavours so successfully dance upon the taste buds.

Such a garnish, with a large steamed sea bass, was my first experience of fine Pekingese cooking – or Bejingese, perhaps, now – soon after I had arrived in London some 30 odd years ago. And it was on Willesden High Road, of all places. Here is its Wikipedia entry:

'The Kuo Yuan was established in 1963 when a group of Chinese restaurateurs managed to convince the Chinese ambassador's chef, a Mr Kuo from Beijing, to defect. A visit by Princess Margaret and Lord Snowdon, the Posh and Becks of their day, put both the restaurant and Chinese food on the map. It was also recommended by Egon Ronay.'

And, as it so happened, it was to be on a visit with Egon Ronay himself (for whom I was working as an inspector at the time) and his friend, the late, legendary Ken Lo, who later went on to open his own restaurants and who had already written several excellent books on Chinese cookery. I recall Egon telling me he had also been a tennis blue at Cambridge.

It was a marvellous evening, with many dishes ordered, including some that would not normally have been offered to gweilos (the Chinese slang for Caucasians). But it was the sea bass I particularly remember, so perfectly cooked as it was, with its pearly-white flesh all moist and juicy, together with an oily dressing of soy and this great pile of just-wilting shredded ginger and spring onions covering the entire fish. It was to be an important initiation to a huge learning curve, that evening, the least of it learning how to prise morsels of fish from the bone with chopsticks.

A pleasing condiment to have around is a ginger-infused vinegar. It is particularly good sprinkled onto a bowl of congee (see page 182), or any other Chinese-inspired dish, simple stir-fried noodles or plain boiled rice, even. You can use white wine vinegar if you like, but I think it is worthwhile searching out rice wine vinegar. For ease of sprinkling, either use an old soy sauce bottle (the ones with a spout on either side of the cap) or an emptied bottle of Sarson's malt vinegar with a sprinkler cap.

One-third fill the chosen receptacle with very finely chopped peeled fresh ginger (a funnel is the easiest way to do this, forcing it through with a chopstick or similar), then top up with vinegar. Leave to infuse for a week or so, shaking it about a bit from time to time, then use the infused vinegar as desired. I think it is delicious sprinkled over scrambled eggs cooked with spring onions, for example, which, after all, is quite apt here.

Oriental spring onion, radish & cucumber salad with cashews & vermicelli

Before you start, you will need to hand both ginger syrup and sesame paste. Also, feel free to add more of one ingredient or another, and to adjust the sweet/sharp balance of the dressing.

Serves 4

100g dried thread vermicelli (or glass noodles)
2 heaped tbsp unsalted cashew nuts (not roasted)
salt
a little sunflower oil
1 bunch of radishes, trimmed
6 spring onions, trimmed
½ large cucumber
generous handful each of coriander and mint leaves, torn
1–2 large red chillies, sliced

for the dressing

1 tbsp ginger syrup (see opposite)
1 tbsp sesame paste (see page 189)
juice of 2 limes
1 tbsp light soy sauce
1 tbsp sesame oil

to garnish

2 tsp toasted sesame seeds

Snap the vermicelli into shorter lengths, one third of the original, folded skein. Soak in cold water for about 30 minutes, or until well softened. Drain and return to the bowl. Now cover with boiling water and fork and lift the noodles around for a few minutes until they have become silky, soft and tender (eat one). Drain, rinse in cold water and set aside.

In a small frying pan, gently toast the cashews with a little salt in a thread of oil until golden all over. Cool, and then crush each cashew lightly with the back of a knife. Reserve.

Cut the radishes into quarters or rounds, the spring onions into diagonal shreds and the cucumber into thick matchsticks. Tip the prepared vegetables into a large bowl and add the vermicelli, coriander, mint and chilli. Mix together with your hands to distribute everything evenly.

Now whisk the dressing ingredients together in a small bowl. Add to the salad and mix together once more with two forks, lifting and dropping the salad so that all is evenly dressed. Pile onto a shallow serving dish and sprinkle over the crushed cashews and sesame seeds. Best eaten pleasantly chilled, with warm sake or ice-cold beer.

Ginger syrup

450g granulated sugar
350ml water
finely pared zest of 1 lemon (use a potato peeler)
150g fresh ginger, peeled and coarsely grated

Dissolve the sugar in the water in a pan over a medium heat, then bring to the boil and cook for 2 minutes. Immediately add the lemon zest and ginger and stir together. Bring back to the boil for a few seconds and then pour into a bowl. Cover and leave to infuse overnight.

The following day, add 2 tbsp water and warm through until liquid and pourable. Strain through a sieve and press on the solids with the back of a ladle to extract all the ginger and lemon flavours. Pour the syrup into a screw-top jar and store in the fridge until needed, where it will keep happily for a several weeks.

A kind of hot & sour soup with tofu

This serves as an almost instant, meat-free version of the famously perky Chinese soup. However, look upon it as a soup in its own right – albeit with a nod or two to the original. It is important to use white pepper here, for its unique flavour and heat.

Serves 4

- 20g dried shitake mushrooms
- 200ml hot water
- 750ml stock
- 125g very thinly sliced leek, mostly the white part
- 1½–2 tbsp black Chinese vinegar, rice vinegar or sherry vinegar, to taste
- 100ml light soy sauce
- 75ml Chinese rice wine
- 1 tbsp fresh ginger julienne strips (fine matchsticks)
- ½ tbsp finely chopped garlic
- 125g frozen sweetcorn kernels
- 125g frozen peas
- 2 tsp freshly ground white pepper
- 150g tofu, cut into small cubes
- 2 tsp arrowroot, slaked with 1 tbsp cold water

to garnish

- sliced spring onions
- sesame oil
- coriander leaves, roughly chopped

First soak the shitake mushrooms in the hot water for 30 minutes, then drain, reserving the liquor for the soup, and slice the shitake. Strain the mushroom liquor through a muslin-lined sieve to remove any grit.

Simmer the leek in the stock and mushroom liquor in a large pan until soft. Add the rest of the ingredients, except the arrowroot and tofu. Bring up to the boil and then simmer for 15 minutes.

Stir in the tofu, followed by the arrowroot, and continue cooking for a few more minutes until the soup is lightly thickened and shiny; don't cook for too long, as arrowroot has a tendency to break down and the soup will thin out.

Decant into hot soup bowls and add a touch of sliced spring onion, sesame oil and chopped coriander to each serving.

A ginger & spring onion dressing for grilled aubergine

The best aubergines for utilising this sweet and sour dressing most successfully are the elongated, pale purple and thin-skinned variety. I have tried the recipe with the common or garden black skinned ones, but with disappointment.

Serves 4

200ml Chinese rice wine
50ml light soy sauce
1 tbsp ginger syrup (see page 94)
20g fresh ginger, peeled and chopped
1 tbsp chopped spring onions
2 garlic cloves, peeled and chopped
1 tbsp rice wine vinegar
2 tsp sesame seeds

to serve

4 large aubergines
oil for shallow or deep-frying
chopped coriander leaves to garnish (optional)

Pour the rice wine into a saucepan, bring up to the boil and ignite. Turn down to a more relaxed simmer and, once the flames have died down, continue to reduce the liquid until about half its original volume. Allow to cool completely, then pour into a small food processor. Add the remaining ingredients and purée until smooth-ish. Pour into a small bowl.

To prepare the aubergines, cut them in half lengthways. Heat the oil in a suitable pan and fry the aubergines for about 10–15 minutes (less if deep-frying), turning as necessary, until nearly tender. Place, cut side down, on kitchen paper to drain well.

Now preheat the grill to medium and lay the aubergine halves in a heatproof dish, cut side uppermost. Slash the surface in a few places with a sharp knife and then spoon over some of the dressing, pushing it down into the aubergine flesh. Grill for a few moments, then add a little more dressing. Continue to grill the aubergines until golden and drenched in dressing; a modicum of residue will also have collected in the dish, which you may allow to become deliciously sticky and aromatic.

Serve two aubergine halves per person and, if desired, garnish with chopped coriander leaves.

Chillies & Avocados

It was on a trip to New York last year that I first met the chef Mario Batali. He had very kindly hosted a splendid dinner at his restaurant Babbo, together with a mutual friend of ours and other jolly guests, too. So, it was a happy party and, as the evening wore on, became positively vivacious. Mario had also laid on some wonderful old Italian wines that included, as far as I remember – and which is difficult – a 1958 Barolo. But the food was splendid and memorable.

One particular dish drew my attention, a braise of squid cooked '... in the style of a Sicilian lifeguard'; 'Could I just have the lifeguard and hold the squid, please?' I quipped. Anyway, Mario said that the squid had been on the menu since Babbo's opening night, 11 years ago, but that he now stirred in a jalapeño chilli relish just before serving the dish. Well, let me tell you, it was just marvellous! The relish recipe follows, and also appears in other chapters. Mario says he loves it so much that he often spreads it thickly on toast.

Learning of this delicious paste further urged me to discover more about jalapeños, now widely available all year round. The flavour of the jalapeño is unlike other green chillies, in that although it is fiery, the flavour emerges as rich and fruity, together with a juiciness that is so often missing in other varieties.

My first look at an avocado was on Christmas morning when aged about six. Mum had bought Dad a hamper from the very grand Kendals department store food hall, in Manchester, for one of his presents. Kendals, then (1960), was possibly the only grocers in the entire northwest of England where an avocado could be purchased. We were all very excited for Dad as, at the time, his cooking skills were becoming more and more exotic. Paella, moules marinières, Indian curries and sweet 'n' sour pork were making regular appearances on family Saturday nights, or when Mum was in dinner party mode. It is little wonder some of this would eventually rub off onto someone else... And I bet you we called it 'advocado'.

Almond & jalapeño relish

Makes about 300ml
50g whole almonds
150g green jalapeño chillies
1 small red onion, peeled
1 tsp Maldon salt
75–100ml extra virgin
olive oil
pinch of sugar

Roughly chop the almonds, chillies and onion and put into a small food processor with the rest of the ingredients. Grind everything together until smooth-ish, but don't take it to an absolute purée. This relish is best eaten or used fresh, the day it is made, but it can be frozen in small pots.

Guacamole

I love this particular method for making guacamole, as it turns out so very green. The inclusion of fresh green tomatillos helps, naturally, but you could use tomatoes instead and forgo the singular, verdant hue.

Serves 2–4, as a snack
1 medium onion, peeled and chopped
juice of 1 small lime, or more
salt
1–2 jalapeño chillies, de-seeded (for less heat) or not, chopped
generous handful of coriander leaves
1–2 tomatillos depending on size (or tomatoes)
2–3 ripe hass avocados, about 500g

Put the onion, lime juice, salt, chillies and coriander into a small food processor and purée until smooth-ish. Tip into a fine sieve suspended over a bowl and force out all the juice from the mulch using the back of a ladle.

Slice the tomatillos and then finely chop them. Halve the avocados, remove the peel and stone, then coarsely chop the flesh. Add the avocados and tomatillos to the onion chilli juice, toss to mix and check for salt.

Chill the guacamole and eat with tortilla chips, naturally. And maybe a Margherita, or two...

Chilled avocado soup with tomatillo salsa

One of the most delicious and delicate cold soups I know – and so very easy to make. The salsa may also be made with tomatoes, of course.

Serves 4

for the salsa

150g tomatillos (or tomatoes)
1 jalapeño chilli, de-seeded (for less heat) or not
½ red onion, peeled
small handful of coriander leaves, chopped
juice of 1 lime, or more
salt
pinch of sugar

for the soup

2–3 ripe, chilled hass avocados
150ml chilled stock, or more to taste
350ml chilled buttermilk
few shakes of green Tabasco
juice of 1 small lime, or more
salt
pinch of cayenne pepper

to finish (optional)

a little soured cream thinned with a little milk

To make the salsa, finely chop the tomatillos (or tomatoes), chilli and onion and put into a bowl. Add the rest of the ingredients and mix everything together. Check the seasoning, adding another squeeze of lime juice if you wish. Leave to macerate while you make the soup.

For the soup, halve the avocados, remove the peel and stone, then coarsely chop the flesh. Place in a blender (preferable to a food processor, here) with all the other ingredients and whiz until very smooth indeed. Even so, I always pass the soup through a fine sieve just to make sure, but then pedantic is my middle name... Put to chill in the fridge for at least 30 minutes, or longer.

If, once chilled, the soup is too thick for your liking, thin with a touch more chilled stock. Taste for seasoning and add a little more lime juice if you think it is needed.

Pour into chilled soup bowls and spoon a small pile of salsa into the centre of each serving. If you like, drizzle with some thinned soured cream, too.

Chilli con carnevale

I am moderately chuffed over the naming of this dish. Carnevale from the Italian/Latin is the original meaning of the word 'carnival': carne 'meat'; vale 'leave'. Or, in other words, 'goodbye meat' on the last day before Lent begins, which is also Shrove Tuesday, and Mardigras: 'Fat Tuesday'. Capiche?

The chilli powder specified in the recipe is not 'pure' chilli powder, or hot cayenne pepper; rather, it is a chilli powder 'mix', which includes oregano and cumin as seasoning ingredients. The one I always use – and with great success – is the readily available Schwartz brand. It is sold as both 'hot' and 'mild', although I prefer the hot variety, and each will provide the correct 'chilli' flavour. Also, I like to add a little more cumin and oregano, too. Together with the jalapeño relish stirred in at the end, it really makes this meatless chilli a memorable one.

Serves 4

3 tbsp olive oil
1 large onion, peeled and chopped
2 celery sticks, peeled and chopped
1 green pepper, de-seeded and chopped
1 red pepper, de-seeded and chopped
2 large flat mushrooms, chopped
4 garlic cloves, peeled, crushed and finely chopped
1 tbsp hot chilli powder
1 tsp ground cumin
½ tsp dried oregano
1 tbsp tomato purée
2 x 420g tins red kidney beans, drained
1 x 420g tin chopped tomatoes
150ml stock
salt
1–2 tbsp almond & jalapeño relish (see page 94)

for garnishing

soured cream
tomato salsa (see page 95)
thinly sliced spring onions

Preheat the oven to 160°C/gas mark 3. Heat the olive oil in a solid cooking pot and add the onion, celery, both peppers, mushrooms and garlic. Fry gently, stirring occasionally, for about 20–30 minutes until well coloured.

Stir in the chilli powder, cumin and oregano, and continue to cook gently for 5 minutes, so 'cooking out' the spices. Add the tomato purée and allow that to sizzle for a few minutes, until it changes colour from bright red to more of a deep rust.

Now tip in the beans, tinned tomatoes and stock. Stir together until well amalgamated and add a little salt (the chilli will reduce somewhat during its cooking time, so beware). Cook, uncovered, in the oven for about

1 hour, taking the pot out a couple of times to gently stir the chilli, while

being careful not to break up the beans.

Remove from the oven and place over a very low heat. You will now notice that the oil has settled on the surface. Well, I like to leave it there and then stir it in, but if you wish for a less oily chilli, then remove it with a few sheets of kitchen paper applied to the surface area. For me, the finished chilli should be fairly thick, so if the mixture remains too sloppy, allow it to reduce until a desired consistency has been reached.

Check for salt and stir in the jalapeño relish, to taste. Serve in individual bowls and add as much or as little garnish as you like.

Pimento & potato stew with jalapeño relish

The jalapeño relish transforms this simple vegetable stew.

Serves 2, generously

350g medium-small potatoes (preferably red-skinned Desiree), peeled
350g red peppers
2 tbsp olive oil
1 medium onion, peeled and sliced
3 garlic cloves, peeled and sliced
1 bay leaf
3 strips of lemon zest
salt
250ml stock
2 tsp almond & jalapeño relish (see page 94), or to taste
a little chopped coriander (optional)

Preheat the oven to 180°C/gas mark 4. Cut the potatoes lengthways into quarters. Core and de-seed the peppers and then cut into pieces similar in size to the potatoes.

In a roomy, lidded cooking pot, heat the olive oil and add the onion. Cook gently until softened and then tip in the potatoes, peppers, garlic, bay, lemon zest and salt to taste. Stir together well and add the stock.

Bring the pot up to a simmer, then cover the vegetables with a piece of greaseproof paper, cut to fit, and put on the lid. Cook in the oven for 40 minutes, or until the potatoes are tender and the red peppers are nice and soft, too.

Stir in the jalapeño relish, being careful not to break up the potatoes, and sprinkle over the chopped coriander, if using. Serve directly from the pot into warmed soup plates. Eat with spoons.

Aubergines & Peppers

Aubergines have always played a big part in my life. I love the look of them, all of them – so much so that an entire shelf in my sitting room is given over to inedible, decorative examples. After many years of generous gifts from friends, with a few found by me, this purple-black corner space is now entirely filled. The only drawback, I guess, is that they take an age to dust...

It has been suggested that the earliest known variety of aubergine is the small white one, hence the name 'eggplant'. Some perfect examples truly resemble a white egg, save the obvious stalk. Other varieties followed, or maybe they were already waiting in the wings, such as the tiny, slightly bitter green pea aubergine and a larger, also white-ish one, about the size of a squash ball, from Thailand. There is also the long, pale purple and deliciously thin-skinned, generally Asian variety – although relatively common in my west London, Middle Eastern grocer's, too. These are absolutely the ones to use for all recipes where the skin is as important as the flesh within, in that it becomes indiscernible, once cooked and eaten (see pages 108–9.)

One of my most favourite is the lilac, purple and creamy giant ball of an aubergine, from Sicily.

Although this is also a fairly thin-skinned variety, in that country (as all Sicilians would have you believe) you would almost never consume a dish of these unpeeled. I approve of this, especially when the vegetable is unadorned, say slices that have been simply grilled or cooked in olive oil, as part of an antipasti. Who needs to eat the skin? Of course, this is even more relevant when using the common, mostly hothouse Dutch-grown black beasts that are all most of us can find. They ain't bad, but they are one dimensional when compared with Sicilian monsters, with which one could almost play football.

Provençal, sun-drenched black-skinned aubergines and similarly ripened red peppers, are just two of the ingredients that go towards the fabrication of a colourful ratatouille. A peerless vegetable dish if ever there was one, which I prefer to eat cold or at least at room temperature. So, why no recipe from this cook? Well, you know, I think I would rather talk it through, this time, rather than list and measure.

One of the best, if not the best, is a ratatouille I have eaten many times at the tiny La Merenda restaurant, in Nice, on a small street running up from the seafront and just by the market. I cannot offer a telephone number, as it does not have one, nor does it accept payment by credit card or cheque.

Dominique Le Stanc, chef-proprietor, makes a ratatouille that he only ever serves in late spring and summer, when all the components are at their very best. He uses red and yellow peppers, small and tender aubergines and courgettes, sweet onions, fabulously ripe tomatoes, which – sensibly – he does not skin, as to so do would allow them to melt away into the dish, as sauce.

I believe that he cooks the ingredients separately, slightly burnishing them in local olive oil, then mixes them together and turns the tomatoes through the other vegetables for just a few minutes until they only just collapse. To finish the dish – and this is his master stroke – a small spoonful of basil, garlic and olive oil, mashed to a paste, is then poured over each plateful. Play around with that, please, won't you?

Caponata

It was either going to be this one, or the ratatouille, that would be given a full recipe or a talk-through. The caponata won by a short head – and it is a little more complicated and has many more ingredients, too.

Serves 4

- 2 large aubergines (the fat, purple and white Sicilian ones if possible)
- salt
- 1 large red onion, peeled, halved and thickly sliced
- 4 celery sticks, peeled, halved lengthways and sliced into small lengths
- 1 small yellow pepper, halved, de-seeded and thickly sliced
- 1 small red pepper, halved, de-seeded and thickly sliced
- 5–6 tbsp olive oil
- 100ml water
- 3 tbsp red wine vinegar
- 1 rounded tbsp sugar
- 2 tsp tomato purée
- 1 tbsp raisins
- about 12 green olives, pitted and halved
- 1 tbsp capers, drained and lightly squeezed dry
- freshly ground white pepper
- 1 tbsp pine kernels

Peel the aubergines and thickly slice into half rounds. Spread them out on a kitchen surface and sprinkle with enough salt to season generously. Gather them up in your hands, mingle together in a colander, place upon a plate and leave to exude their juices for at least 40 minutes.

Meanwhile, using a frying pan, and in four separate stages, quietly stew the onion, celery, yellow and red peppers separately, each in 1 tbsp of the olive oil, until softened and only just coloured. For the fifth stage, wash and dry the aubergines and similarly soften in olive oil. Place all five vegetables in a bowl and mingle together.

Now add the water, vinegar, sugar, tomato purée and raisins to the frying pan. Bring to the boil and simmer for several minutes until lightly thickened and the raisins have plumped somewhat. Stir in the olives and capers and tip the entire contents of the pan into the bowl of vegetables.

Gently heat the pine kernels in a dry frying pan until golden brown. Add them to the caponata, season with pepper to taste and check for salt. Lubricate with a little more olive oil if you think it warrants it and serve at room temperature.

Red pepper mousse with garlic toasts

The main reason I suggest using Spanish piquillo peppers from a jar in this recipe, is that their flavour is more intense than those of fresh ones that have been baked and peeled by you. Okay, it also makes the job easier... But it is the taste that remains paramount, here. Be sure to remove any little black bits from the peppers if they have been char-grilled, before processing.

Serves 4–5

for the mousses

150g ripe tomatoes, coarsely chopped
1 rounded tbsp agar flakes
150g (drained weight) Spanish piquillo peppers from a jar
pinch of cayenne pepper
½ tsp celery salt
½ tsp sugar
1 tsp red wine vinegar
125ml whipping cream

for the garlic toasts

allow 2 long slices of rustic baguette (cut on the diagonal), per person
1 garlic clove, peeled and halved
Maldon salt and freshly ground pepper
olive oil for brushing

Place the tomatoes in a small pan and sprinkle over the agar flakes. Warm through over a low heat, swirling the tomatoes around until they begin to wilt and release some of their juices, before stirring in the slowly melting agar flakes. Allow to stew gently for a further 3–4 minutes.

Purée the piquillo peppers, cayenne, celery salt, sugar and vinegar in a blender until very smooth. Add the tomatoes to the blender now (scraping out every last vestige with a spatula) and blend briefly once more. Now pass this mixture through a fine sieve into a bowl, pressing down on the solids with the back of a small ladle. Place in the fridge for at least 30–40 minutes, or until beginning to set.

Whip the cream in another bowl, only just until soft peaks form. Now transfer the whisk to the pepper mixture and give this a brief whisking to loosen it. Carefully fold the cream into the pepper purée until well combined and without any white streaks. Decant into ramekins, smooth over the surface and stretch a piece of cling film over the top of each one. Place in the fridge to set, for at least 2 hours, or longer.

For the garlic toasts, toast the baguette slices until nicely burnished. Rub the cut garlic clove over each one, season lightly and brush with olive oil.

Eat the red pepper mousse with teaspoons, occasionally spreading some of it onto the garlic toasts.

Fried aubergine with skordalia

The very nicest of Greek taverna dishes, best enjoyed over a late lunch and with some very cold, iced ouzo.

Serves 2

1 large aubergine, trimmed
salt
flour for coating
olive oil for shallow-frying

for the skordalia

50g crustless, slightly stale fresh white bread, in large cubes
150ml milk
1 garlic clove, peeled and crushed to a paste with salt
1–2 scant tbsp white wine vinegar
pepper
about 50ml olive oil

Slice the aubergine into rounds, about 1.5cm thick. Immerse in a bowl of well-salted water and leave to soak for 30 minutes, turning the slices around from time to time.

Meanwhile, make the skordalia. Soak the bread in the milk for a few minutes until spongy. Squeeze the excess milk out with your hands and put the bread into a food processor with the garlic, vinegar and some pepper. Pulse briefly, adding the olive oil in a thin stream, until the mixture is thick and paste-like; try not to overwork it, however, as you want to retain some of the texture of the bread.

Drain the aubergine slices in a colander, then lay out on a tea towel in one layer, but don't let them dry out; they should remain a bit wet. Now heat about a 1cm depth of olive oil in a large frying pan until hot, but not smoking. Dip each slice of aubergine in flour, shake off excess and fry about 5–6 slices at a time, turning once, until golden brown on each side. Drain on kitchen paper.

Serve the crisp-fried aubergine slices piping hot, with the skordalia.

Grilled aubergine with pesto

An old favourite, which I could not resist including here.

Serves 2

1 large aubergine
about 100ml extra virgin olive oil
salt and freshly ground pepper
3 tbsp pine kernels
a large bunch of basil
3 garlic cloves, peeled and crushed
3 tbsp freshly grated pecorino or Parmesan cheese
½ lemon

Preheat the oven to 220°C/gas mark 7. Cut the aubergine lengthways in half, through the stalk. Using a small, sharp knife, make a criss-cross pattern across the cut surfaces, to a depth of about 2cm. Brush with a little of the olive oil and season. Bake in the oven for 20–30 minutes. The flesh should be very soft.

Meanwhile, lightly toast the pine kernels in a dry frying pan, then remove from the pan and cool. Process the basil, garlic and pine kernels, together with a little salt and pepper, to a paste in a food processor (or use a pestle and mortar for a more authentic result). Now add enough of the olive oil to produce a loose textured purée. Finally, briefly mix in the cheese.

Spread the pesto over the scored surfaces of the aubergine and grill until golden and bubbling. Serve with a squeeze of lemon.

Potatoes Old & New

Triple-cooked chips, albeit delicious, are nothing more than chips cooked with a great deal of care. Why does one need to be told they are triple-cooked? The same goes for 'hand-cut' chips. Why does one need this information? Maybe restaurant kitchens want us to be wildly impressed with all of this. Just get on with the cutting and cooking is what I say.

All good chips need to be cooked twice anyway, to make them crisp: first slow-fried in oil at a low temperature for several minutes, then finished in hot oil for about two. You can leave a few hours between these stages if that suits your timing better.

When I first learnt how to do this as a teenage apprentice, it reminded me of my brother and I, years before, making chips in our chip-pan at home and realising that we could have made them much nicer than we did, had we known this trick at the time. Our chips, then, emerged limp, a deep brown on the outside and always a little bit raw in the middle. But we ate them anyway, because using the chip pan at all was fun, exciting and just a little bit dangerous.

Conversely, in terms of crispness and texture, one would never want the initial rustle of a chip-shop chip to last. The great joy of such a morsel is its wane from the fryer – so becoming deliciously warm and only just tinged with tiny, remaining edges of crunch – helped, of course, by having been drenched in copious shakes of malt vinegar.

Bringing some excellent fish and chips home once, and not having the Sarson's bottle to hand, I made the heinous mistake of using tarragon vinegar instead, this being my only choice from the store-cupboard. So horrible they were, that they ended up in the bin after only a couple of bites. Should have known better. Silly me.

Fragrantly, spring moving into summertime arrives for me with the first scent from a pan of new potatoes simmering with mint. So good are these tiny little marbles, once buttered, that I can eat a bowl of them all on their own – vegetarian food at its very best, I claim. When something so simple as this tastes so very good, it does not need any faffing around with – the purity should be championed.

Early Cornish and Pembrokeshire new potatoes are personal favourites, with Jerseys, I feel, now too overproduced. As for the absurdly early ones that appear on the market, even in March sometimes, these have clearly been grown under poly-tunnels and should be avoided – especially at the prices asked for them. Naturally, if you are lucky enough to be on the island of Jersey itself, and know of a small organic producer who still uses the local seaweed as fertiliser, then this is entirely another matter.

Simple new potato salad

It is important, here, to dress the potatoes while they are still warm. Any leftover dressing will keep well in the fridge.

Serves 4

700g new potatoes, washed
salt
for the dressing
2 tbsp smooth Dijon mustard
2 tbsp white wine or tarragon vinegar
salt and freshly ground pepper
2 tbsp lukewarm water
325ml sunflower oil
2 tbsp snipped chives or spring onions
1 tbsp finely chopped parsley

Put the potatoes to simmer (or steam) in salted water. When cooked through, drain and leave until just cool enough to handle, then peel.

To make the dressing, put the mustard, vinegar, seasoning and water in a blender or food processor and whiz until smooth, then start adding the oil in a thin stream. When the consistency is pale and creamy, have a taste.

If you think it is too thick, add a little more water; the consistency should be one almost of salad cream.

Slice the potatoes into a roomy bowl, sprinkle over the spring onions and parsley and add enough dressing to thoroughly coat (but not drown) the potatoes, turning them gently.

Baked new potatoes & new season's garlic

Only use the larger, mid-season new potatoes for this dish; the really early ones are too small and waxy.

Serves 2
150ml white wine
2–3 tbsp extra virgin
olive oil
500g medium new potatoes, peeled and halved
1 head of new season's garlic, cloves peeled and halved
2–3 bay leaves, torn
salt and freshly ground pepper

Preheat the oven to 160°C/gas mark 3. Put the wine into a lidded, heavy-based cooking pot in which you will cook the potatoes (packed in fairly tightly). Bring to the boil and ignite. Once the flames have dissipated, add the olive oil and potatoes and then tuck in the garlic and bay, here and there. Season and bring to a simmer. Put on the lid and bake in the oven for at least 1 hour, or until the potatoes are very tender.

Mum's potato cakes

We kept seconds of these warm in front of a roaring coal fire in our house. And it was always the same glass Pyrex dish that was used for cold and dark, wintry Sunday afternoon potato cakes. I'm not sure, now, whether they would taste quite the same if dished up out of anything else. I can still see the remains of liquid, golden butter glimpsed through the glass, the fire's glowing embers reflected upon its molten surface.

Serves 4, for tea

600–700g potatoes (Desiree, for preference), peeled and cut into chunks
salt and freshly ground white pepper
about 100–120g plain flour
vegetable oil
plenty of butter, to serve

Warm the oven in advance and put an ovenproof serving dish inside to warm up. Steam (for preference) or boil the potatoes in salted water until tender. If boiled, drain well and dry out in the pan over a low heat for a few minutes.

Tip the cooked potatoes into a roomy pan, then immediately mash until fluffy but not super-smooth by any means. Tip out onto a work surface or tray and allow to cool and dry out for about half an hour.

Once ready to handle, sprinkle the potato with salt and grind over the pepper. Now, little by little, sift over the flour, working it into the potato with your fingers using a gentle kneading movement, until the mixture is workable but with a slight trace of stickiness. You will almost certainly need the full 100g, maybe a little more.

Roll out to about 1.5cm thick and then cut into cakes the size of small scones. Take a frying pan, add a little oil and gently heat. Dust each cake with a little flour and begin to fry them, 3 or 4 at a time. Do this ever so quietly until pale golden, about 3 minutes on each side. Slide them directly into the warmed serving dish and put it back into the oven to keep the potato cakes warm while you finish cooking the rest.

Once they are all cooked, cut slices of butter directly from the packet and place one upon each potato cake. By the time you serve them, the butter will have reached that perfect moment of half-melted. You will need a small plate, a fork and big napkins.

Potato pie with Beaufort cheese

A most luxurious and rich dish, here, for that which is, essentially, nothing more than potatoes in pastry.

Serves 4

500g medium potatoes (Desiree, for preference), washed
salt and freshly ground pepper
100ml double cream
2 garlic cloves, lightly bruised
25–30g butter
375g ready-made puff pastry, in 2 equal sheets
75g Beaufort cheese, very thinly sliced
½ tsp thyme leaves
beaten egg, to glaze the pastry

Preheat the oven to 200°C/gas mark 6. Steam (for preference) or boil the potatoes in salted water until tender, then cool and peel. Slice moderately thickly and put to one side.

Place the cream in a saucepan with the garlic, bring to the boil, then take off the heat, cover and leave to infuse.

Put a flat baking sheet into the oven. Lightly smear another one with some of the butter. Roll out one puff pastry sheet thinly, to a 2–3mm thickness, and lay it on the buttered baking sheet. Mark a circle on it, about 20cm in diameter. Cover the pastry round with half of the potatoes, arranging them in a slightly overlapping layer within the circle. Lightly season and cover with half the cheese and thyme leaves, adding a few flecks of butter. Repeat these layers. Brush the pastry edges with beaten egg.

Roll out the other sheet of pastry as above and then place over the filling. Clamp down the edges with your fingers and then trim to a round, using a flan ring that is slightly larger than 20cm as a guide.

Now, brush the pastry all over with egg and, using the tines of a fork, decorate the edge. Make a small hole in the centre of the pie, about 5mm in diameter. Remove the garlic from the cream and, using a small funnel, slowly pour the infused cream into the pie through the hole, allowing it to settle inside before adding more. Once it is quite clear that no more cream will fit, stop pouring; you may have a modicum left.

Slide the pie into the oven, onto the preheated baking sheet. Bake for about 20 minutes, then turn the oven setting down to 180°C/gas mark 4. Continue cooking for a further 20 minutes, or until crisp and nicely puffed; if the pie is browning too quickly, cover loosely with a sheet of foil.

Let the pie stand for a good 10 minutes out of the oven before serving. Cut into wedges and eat with a crisp green salad or just on its own.

Chicory & Watercress

I have often wondered whether everyone experiences difficulty with eating bitter salad leaves until they are, at least, into their late teens – or even a touch older. They are, possibly, an acquired taste at any time of life, but as with cooked spinach, once adolescence is behind one, these astringent notes have a tendency to creep up and delight the taste buds.

Too many times have I told the story of being almost force fed chicory and its relatives by chef, when an apprentice teenage cook, but the occasion was certainly a watershed moment for me. It didn't mean that I suddenly wanted to search out bagfuls of chicory every single day after that, but the seeds of a lifelong love of the stuff had, most definitely, been sown.

My earliest preference was for cooked chicory – or endive, or witloof (to use the Flemish) – and remains so. I read many recipes for the cooking or braising of chicory and it seems to me that those who have chosen to enlighten the reader would have it that they enjoy the vegetable a touch al dente. Well, this is hardly the point; either the chicory is well cooked right through until soft, or it is eaten raw. Both undeniably delicious. But to dither between the two is just playing silly beggars.

The finest watercress I have eaten was in Dublin, of all places. The good folk of that fair city might well admonish me for that declaration of surprise, but it is simply that I wasn't expecting it. The unpretentious restaurant that offered it to me was a very good operation and given to serving generous portions at kind prices, but the quality of those bright and bountiful leaves was nothing short of shocking. Truthfully, I had never seen or tasted watercress like it.

The size of each sprig, and so perfectly trimmed and picked over, was double – or maybe even treble – the dimensions of perfectly serviceable, English watercress from Hampshire, maybe. Combined with slivers of roast chicken, shallots and a very fine vinaigrette, these verdant leaves made a delightful composition.

Watercress & turnip soup

Two slightly bitter ingredients, which surprisingly, when cooked together seem to cancel each other out, resulting in a soup of sweet subtlety.

Serves 4

40g butter
175g leeks, white part only, sliced and washed
250g turnips, peeled and diced
2–3 bunches of watercress, about 300g, washed and coarsely chopped
500ml stock
a little grated nutmeg
salt and freshly ground pepper
250ml milk
75ml whipping cream

Melt the butter in a roomy pot, add the leeks and cook gently until softened. Tip in the turnips, stir around for a few minutes, put on the lid and allow the two vegetables to quietly stew together for about 5 minutes. Uncover, stir in the watercress and let it wilt into the leeks and turnip.

Pour in the stock, lightly season with nutmeg, salt and pepper, then bring up to a gentle simmer and replace the lid. Cook for about 20 minutes, or until the turnips are very tender. Stir in the milk and bring back to a simmer. Check the seasoning and then purée the soup in a blender until smooth. Pass through a fine sieve, stir in the cream and gently reheat. Particularly nice with some tiny, buttery croûtons.

Watercress & curly endive salad with croûtons

Curly endive and watercress marry together extremely well. The bitter of endive and the peppery qualities of watercress might, you think, argue with one another. But no, the pairing produces a harmonious assembly of rare subtlety.

Serves 4, generously

- 2–3 large handfuls of large croûtons, cut from a stale baguette and further left to dry out
- 2 curly endive, trimmed of all outer, dark green leaves, well washed and dried
- 2 bunches of watercress, picked into nice sprigs, washed

for the dressing

- 1 tbsp red wine vinegar
- 2–3 tbsp hot water
- 2 garlic cloves, peeled and crushed to a paste
- salt and freshly ground pepper
- 4–5 tbsp walnut oil
- 3–4 tbsp olive oil

To make the dressing, put the vinegar, hot water, garlic, salt and plenty of pepper into a large salad bowl. Whisk together to dissolve the salt, add the oils and continue whisking until the dressing is loosely emulsified.

To assemble, tip the croûtons into the dressing and deftly mix together with salad servers, coating them well. Allow some of the dressing to soak in for a moment or two, then add the endive and watercress. Mix everything together thoroughly, lifting the croûtons up through the leaves, and serve at once.

Gratin of chicory with mustard sauce

Rich, I believe, might be the word, here.

Serves 4 as a first course, or 2 as a light supper dish

8 small, or 4 large heads of chicory
40g butter
salt and freshly ground pepper
juice of ½ lemon
75ml dry vermouth
2 tsp Pernod (optional)
100ml stock
150ml double cream
2 tsp smooth Dijon mustard
1 tbsp fine, fresh white breadcrumbs
1 tbsp freshly grated Parmesan

Trim the chicory of any damaged leaves and remove the conical core from the base of each with a sharp knife. Melt the butter in a shallow pan and cook until foaming. Put in the chicory, turning them thoroughly in the butter, and season lightly. Turn the heat down to low and gently colour the chicory on all sides until glossy and pale golden.

Add the lemon juice, vermouth and Pernod, if using, and bring up to a simmer. Allow to bubble away until the liquid has reduced by about half, then turn the chicory over and add the stock. Continue simmering, uncovered, for a further 30–40 minutes, or until the chicory is tender when pierced with a sharp knife at its thickest point. Remove the chicory to a gratin dish and keep warm. Heat a radiant grill to medium.

Simmer the juices until syrupy and well flavoured, then stir in the cream. Whisk together, simmer until lightly thickened and then whisk in the mustard. Pour over the chicory, coating them well with the sauce.

Mix together the breadcrumbs and Parmesan, carefully sprinkle over the length of each chicory and slide under the lowest part of the grill, to gently gild. Serve at once, perhaps with some crusty baguette to mop up the delicious sauce.

Wilted radicchio with green sauce

Try to find the long variety of radicchio rather than the more familiar – but more readily available, it must be said – round ones. This, more than anything else, is for the look of the thing, but I think they have a better, bitter flavour, and are more fleshy, too. Note that this dish needs to be started the day before you wish to eat it.

Serves 2

3 large heads of radicchio, about 300–350g
500ml water
150ml red wine vinegar
2 tsp Maldon salt
1 very small onion, peeled and thinly sliced into rings
1–2 tbsp extra virgin olive oil
freshly ground pepper

for the green sauce

small bunch of parsley, leaves only
10 basil leaves
10 mint leaves
1 garlic clove, peeled and crushed
2 tsp Dijon mustard
2 tsp capers, drained and squeezed of excess vinegar
100–120ml extra virgin olive oil
2 hard-boiled eggs, sliced
salt and freshly ground pepper

Cut the radicchio heads vertically into quarters, through the root. Bring the water to the boil in a saucepan with the vinegar and salt added. Taking 3 or 4 quarters of radicchio at a time, plunge them into the boiling liquid for a minute or two, then drain in a colander and lay out on a tea towel to dry for a few minutes.

Lay the radicchio in a dish, scatter over the onion, spoon over the olive oil and grind on some pepper. Gently mix together, cover, and leave in the fridge overnight. When you wish to serve the radicchio, remove it from the fridge a good hour beforehand.

To make the green sauce, put the herbs, garlic, mustard and capers into a small food processor with 2–3 tbsp of the oil. Process for a few seconds, until the solids are only coarsely chopped and then slowly add the rest of the oil in a thin stream until the sauce is thick-ish and very green, but loose of texture and almost more like a dressing.

Serve the radicchio with the sliced eggs and green sauce alongside, and with plenty of warm, crusty baguette.

Spinach & Sorrel

There are two timely ways of preparing spinach, which sit at either end of its cooking spectrum and yet are equally delectable. The first – involving minimal contact with hot butter and stir-frying – is as brief as can be, whereas the second – slow stewing – almost reduces the spinach to rags. Some would say that the latter has been horribly overcooked, especially if they have only ever tasted the former, but I think they would be wrong, here.

Chez Lipp, on the boulevard Saint Germain, in Paris offers a slowly roasted – almost braised, in fact – dish of veal known as a fricandeau, for a delicious Sunday lunchtime plat du jour. There are two choices of accompaniment to the dish: epinards ou lasagnettes. Well, I have never eaten the lasagnettes (presumably some buttery folds of slightly more diminutive sheets of pasta than the usual lasagne), plumping always for the epinards, ever since the first time I tasted it well over 20 years ago. And the dish has possibly been on offer, Chez Lipp, for double or even triple that time, so little does the menu change at this venerable institution.

Even I was surprised when this olive-coloured slop arrived in its white oval dish, looking as if it had simply been emptied out of some ancient can. But the flavour, the flavour! Much butter had clearly been used in its preparation, together with judicious seasoning including a healthy rasp of nutmeg. Occasionally on these Sundays, when not indulging in a first course (which is rare, for me), I ask for seconds of both the veal and the spinach which are always gladly given, albeit with a winsome shrug.

I have often wondered whether this Lipp way with spinach is related to an extraordinary recipe in Elizabeth David's *French Country Cooking*, called Les Epinards du Chanoine Chévrier. The spinach leaves are finely chopped and cooked over a period of 5 days! Amounts of butter are added each day, resulting in a copious '10½oz of butter incorporated...' by the time the dish is finally ready. Even if you find that amount of fat added to 'at least 2–3lb of (uncooked) spinach' deeply shocking and dangerously unhealthy, you should at least try the recipe once. It is both unusual and wildly delicious.

And so to lovely sorrel. I never understand quite why this sharp and tender summer leaf/herb is not more widely available, in season. It collapses and reduces even more swiftly than spinach when cooked, transforming to a muddy green in an instant, yet its mildly acidic flavour is delicate and charming. Do try the creamy sorrel soup (see page 119) and the equally delicious omelette (see page 121).

Spinach mousse with Parmesan cream

Smooth and seductive. A dainty dish.

Serves 4
for the mousse
a little softened butter
250g spinach leaves
2 large eggs
225ml double cream
salt and freshly ground pepper
freshly grated nutmeg

for the Parmesan cream
250ml whipping cream
40–50g Parmesan, freshly grated
salt and freshly ground white pepper

Preheat the oven to 180°C/gas mark 4. Butter the base of each of four buttered dariole moulds or ramekins and line with a tiny disc of greaseproof paper. Blanch the spinach in boiling water for 1–2 minutes. Drain and refresh under very cold running water, then squeeze in a tea towel until completely dry. (You should have approximately 120g cooked weight of spinach.)

Purée the eggs and spinach in a blender until really smooth. Pour into a bowl, stir in the cream until well mixed and season with a little salt, pepper and nutmeg. Pour the mixture into the prepared moulds, filling them to the brim.

Cover each with a round of foil and place in a deep baking dish. Pour tap-hot water into the dish until it comes at least three-quarters of the way up the sides of the moulds. Bake in the oven for 20–25 minutes, or until firm to the touch.

To make the Parmesan cream, pour the cream into a saucepan and whisk in 40g of the Parmesan. Bring to a simmer and allow to gently bubble for a few minutes, whisking occasionally. Taste the sauce and add more cheese if you think it needs it, maybe a little salt, but definitely grind in some pepper. Simmer until of a suitable coating consistency.

Once the mousses are cooked, turn them out onto warmed plates and spoon over the Parmesan cream. Serve promptly.

Iced potage Germiny

This is a light, yet creamy soup, both sharp and refreshing. Don't be upset that the sorrel quickly turns a muddy green colour when cooked, as that is simply what it does.

Serves 4–6
1 litre stock
6 large egg yolks
250ml whipping cream
salt and freshly ground white pepper
500g sorrel, stalks removed and well chopped
juice of ½ lemon
finely snipped chives, to serve

Bring 850ml of the stock to the boil in a roomy pan, then turn the heat down to the merest simmer. Whisk together the egg yolks and cream with some seasoning. Now, wash the whisk and start to gently move it through the stock in a circular motion. At a regular pace, whisk the stock, adding the egg and cream liaison at the same time in a thin stream.

Let the soup cook very gently, stirring with a wooden spoon as if making custard. But, like custard, it can easily curdle, so watch out. The result should be limpid, smooth and the consistency of thin cream. Immediately remove from the heat and liquidise in a blender. Pour into a bowl.

Now heat the remaining 150ml of stock in a non-reactive or stainless steel pan. When boiling, add the sorrel and briefly cook until thoroughly wilted. Add to the soup and stir in well, together with the lemon juice. Cool and chill in the fridge for at least 4 hours.

Check the seasoning and ladle the soup into chilled bowls. Serve sprinkled with the snipped chives.

Spinach & ricotta pancakes

Italian crespelle, to reveal their original provenance. The amount of batter will produce a few more pancakes than needed, but it is impractical to make less. I suggest that you cook extra pancakes and freeze them for another occasion.

Serves 4

for the pancake batter
100g plain flour
2 large eggs
large pinch of salt
250ml milk
50g butter, melted and cooled until tepid, plus a little extra for cooking

for the béchamel sauce
500ml milk
1 bay leaf
salt
60g butter
35g plain flour
freshly ground white pepper

for the filling
750g spinach
75g fresh ricotta cheese
2 large egg yolks
100g Parmesan, freshly grated
salt and freshly ground pepper
freshly grated nutmeg, to taste

to finish
2 tbsp freshly grated Parmesan

To make the pancake batter, whisk the flour, eggs, salt and half the milk together in a bowl until smooth. Add the melted butter and enough of the remaining milk to achieve a thin, pouring cream consistency. Leave to stand for 30 minutes.

To make the béchamel sauce, heat the milk with the bay and a little salt. Simmer for a few minutes, then cover and set aside to infuse off the heat. In another pan, melt the butter and stir in the flour. Cook gently for a minute or two to make a roux, but on no account allow it to colour. Discard the bay leaf and add the milk to the roux, vigorously whisking until smooth. Set the sauce to cook on the lowest possible heat, preferably using a heat-diffuser mat. Stir, fairly constantly, using a wooden spoon and cook for about 15–20 minutes. The sauce will soon become silky and smooth. Add pepper, check for salt, switch off the heat and cover with a tight-fitting lid; this helps to prevent a skin forming. Keep warm.

Preheat the oven to 200°C/gas mark 6. For the filling, blanch the spinach in boiling water for a couple of minutes. Drain and refresh under very cold running water. Squeeze in a tea towel until completely dry. Put the spinach, ricotta, egg yolks, Parmesan, seasoning and nutmeg in a food processor and briefly process to a coarse purée. Spread out on a shallow tray, cover with cling film and chill for a bit, to firm up.

For the pancakes, use a 20cm frying pan. Melt a small amount of butter in the pan and allow it to become hot and sizzling, then pour in enough batter to thinly cover the base of the pan. Cook until the underside is golden, then toss or turn and cook the second side. The first pancake is often a bit of a mess, so you will probably need to chuck it out and then start afresh. Make 8 pancakes and put on one side.

To complete the dish, place 2 tablespoonfuls of the filling on each pancake and roll up, tucking in the ends if necessary. Lay in a lightly buttered baking dish, with space in between each one, then carefully spoon over the béchamel sauce, allowing it to fall into the gaps (this is so the pancakes will be nicely revealed, once the dish has been baked). Sprinkle over the Parmesan and bake in the oven for 30–35 minutes, or until bubbling well and the surface is golden and crusted. Hand extra grated Parmesan at table, if you wish.

Sorrel & soured cream omelette with chives

Quite delicious eaten with a simple new potato salad (see page 106).

Serves 1

30g butter
generous handful of sorrel leaves, trimmed of stalks
salt and freshly ground pepper
3 large eggs
scant 1 tbsp soured cream
1 tsp snipped chives

Melt half the butter in a small pan, add the sorrel leaves and season lightly. Stew until soft and turning a muddy green colour, then cook briskly until almost all the moisture has been driven off. Tip onto a plate and keep warm.

Beat the eggs with the soured cream, add the chives and season lightly. In a favourite omelette pan, heat the remaining butter until foaming and then tip in the egg mixture. Cook the omelette in the usual way and, when almost ready, spoon over the stewed sorrel, flip over and turn onto a warmed plate.

Beetroot & Turnips

One of my earliest memories of delicious food is a deep white dish of sweet and small, tender whole beetroots, served buried in a parsley sauce – their bleeding, ruby juices seeping out beneath their green-flecked blanket. Unusually, for me and my regular memoirist moments of Mum's cooking, this particular treat, for once, was not home-grown, but eaten in an old-fashioned hotel on the banks of Windermere, in The Lake District.

This was in the days when a typical hotel Sunday lunch involved all kinds of vegetables to accompany at least three different roasts, with maybe a seasonal lake fish, too, such as the now increasingly rare Arctic char. Admittedly, there was a habit of overcooking some vegetables, such as cabbage and sprouts (though I would still rather have a soft sprout than a hard green bullet). However, this was compensated by the most wonderful roast potatoes and parsnips, both of which benefited from being overcooked to a crisp. But those beetroots were cooked by someone who really knew.

Beets and turnips – and swedes, too – are very much part of our winter fare (I have slipped in a swede recipe, here, as it is a relative, after all), and I will always adore home-cooked fresh beetroots, sliced while still warm and splashed with malt vinegar. The larger turnip may be peeled and mashed in exactly the same way as the more usual swede, though turnips can sometimes benefit from being blanched once in boiling water, refreshed and then boiled till tender, as traces of bitterness can occasionally be noted. Other countries, however, can turn the common turnip into something quite ingenious.

Although I had first been taken to eat Cantonese dim sum as a trainee Egon Ronay inspector in 1977, at Joy King Lau, just off London's Leicester Square, it took nearly 20 years before I was to be convinced of the delights of fried turnip cakes. I don't quite know why they had previously eluded me. In truth I had seen many Chinatown dim sum trolleys laden down with these little square slabs, ready to be fry-griddled on specially integrated, portable stove tops, but I would always refuse a serving, however pushy the waitress – and they can surely push when offering their wares. I guess there were always just too many other good things with which I wanted to stuff my face.

So, it was not until Hong Kong, in 1996, that my friend Michelle Garnaut generously treated members of her family and friends to lunch at one of the city's most famously good dim sum establishments. Happily, this was on the day following a celebration of her 40th birthday, and with all participants fully aware that lots of good dim sum can magically cure the most severe of hangovers. This particular place also happened to excel at fried turnip cake, so a slice was gently forced upon me. It was a revelation… I have been an addict ever since.

Beetroot jelly with dill & horseradish cream

Delicately sweet and melting on the tongue. The horseradish is a nicely fiery foil, too.

Serves 4

500g cooked beetroot, peeled, plus a little extra, cut into tiny cubes, for garnish (optional)
750ml stock
1 tsp caster sugar
4 heaped tsp agar flakes

for the cream

75g peeled fresh horseradish
1 tbsp soured cream
2 tsp sugar
a little salt
2 tsp lemon juice
150ml whipping cream
2 tsp finely chopped dill

Grate the beetroot and put it into a stainless steel pan, together with 500ml of the stock and the sugar. Bring up to a low simmer and cook, covered, for 10 minutes.

Meanwhile, pour the remaining stock into another, smaller pan. Sprinkle over the agar flakes and allow them to slowly soak into the liquid, then warm through, stirring occasionally, until the flakes have dissolved, about 10 minutes. Pour into the beetroot pan and stir all together.

Now pour the mixture through a sieve set over a bowl and allow it to drip through. Do not force the mixture or it will cloud the liquid; unlike non-vegetarian gelatine, however, there will rarely be a crystal-clear set.

Now take the beetroot liquid and place it over a larger bowl filled with ice cubes and water. Taking a metal spoon, gently stir the liquid around until it just begins to gel – about 10 minutes, or sooner. At this point, if liked, the extra garnish of tiny beetroot cubes may be folded in, but when the mixture starts to gel, it will happen quite swiftly, so be alert.

Spoon the jelly into 4 small glass beakers (best for the look of the thing) or ramekins, but leave enough room for the horseradish cream that will sit on top. Place in the fridge to set for about 1 hour.

To make the cream, finely grate the horseradish – the tears, the tears! Mix with the remaining ingredients, except the dill, and leave to infuse for a few minutes, then pass through a sieve into a bowl, pressing down well to force out as much flavour from the horseradish as possible. Stir in the dill and check for seasoning; it should be nicely nose-cleansingly hot.

Once the jellies have set, spoon a layer of horseradish cream on top and serve. Eat slowly with teaspoons, savouring every mouthful. I like to eat this entirely on its own.

Swede & potato cakes with black pepper cream sauce

The addition of agar flakes is an option here, to help firm up a mixture that can veer towards wetness. However, if you can achieve a thorough drying out of the cooked vegetables, agar flakes should not be necessary.

Serves 4

500g swede
300g potatoes
25g butter
1 tsp Maldon salt
2 tsp agar flakes (optional)
1 large egg yolk
1 tbsp freshly grated Parmesan
1 tbsp chopped spring onion
flour for coating
olive oil for frying

for the sauce

250ml double cream
2 tsp black peppercorns, cracked or coarsely crushed
salt, to taste
30g butter
2 tsp smooth Dijon mustard

to garnish (optional)

watercress sprigs

Preheat the oven to 160°C/gas mark 3. Peel the swede and potatoes and cut them into chunks. Melt the butter in a lidded, roomy pot over a low heat and add the swede, potatoes and salt. Stir together and gently cook for about 5 minutes; more than anything else, this is to coat the vegetables with butter and to get the pot hot. Put on the lid, transfer to the oven and cook for about 45 minutes to 1 hour until the vegetables are tender.

Now return the pot to a very low heat on top of the stove and stir the vegetables around to try and rid them of excess moisture; it does not matter if they colour very slightly, or if they break up a little, either. Mash the vegetables coarsely (an old-fashioned manual masher is best, here) and, if uncertain about wetness, now is the time to sprinkle over the agar flakes and mix them in. Tip into a bowl and allow to cool completely before mixing in the egg yolk, Parmesan and spring onion. Spread on a flat tray and put in the fridge to firm up.

Meanwhile, make the simple sauce. Whisk all the ingredients together in a small pan and bring to a simmer. Cook until slightly thickened and pour into a hot jug or sauceboat.

Form the swede and potato mash into 8 small cakes and roll in flour to coat all over. Heat a little olive oil in a frying pan and gently fry the swede and potato cakes on both sides until golden; drain on kitchen paper.

Serve garnished with sprightly sprigs of chilled watercress, if desired, handing the sauce around separately.

Turnip gratin with cream cheese & Parmesan

Really a lighter version of gratin dauphinois… made with turnips.

Serves 2
1 garlic clove, peeled and crushed
100ml double cream
150ml milk
3 thyme sprigs
250g small turnips
50g cream cheese
a little softened butter
1 tbsp freshly grated Parmesan

Preheat the oven to 180°C/gas mark 4. Put the garlic, cream, milk and thyme into a saucepan and bring to a simmer. Switch off the heat, cover and allow the flavourings to infuse for 5 minutes. Meanwhile, peel the turnips and thinly slice them, preferably on a mandolin.

Strain the creamy milk through a sieve into a bowl and then whisk in the cream cheese. Tip in the sliced turnips and mix well – hands, to be frank, are best, here – whilst also separating the turnip slices from each other.

Lightly butter a presentable baking dish and tip in the turnips and cream, scraping out every last scrap with a spatula. Smooth over the surface and sprinkle with Parmesan. Slide into the oven and bake for 40–50 minutes, turning down the temperature to 160°C/gas mark 3 towards the end of cooking if the surface is colouring too much; a sheet of foil loosely tented over the dish can help, too.

Leave the gratin to stand for 10 minutes before eating. A judiciously dressed, simple green salad on the side is appropriate here.

Oriental fried turnip paste

Those familiar with turnip paste will know that it contains such ingredients as Chinese dried shrimp and bacon; once fried, it is also very enjoyable with a finishing slick of oyster sauce. I decided that I ought to be able to fashion a vegetarian version, even though traditional aficionados might be horrified by such a thought. I urge you to try it – guinea pig gourmet chums simply couldn't get enough. Although a lengthy and slightly complicated recipe, it is well worth the effort. You will need sesame paste (see page 169) to hand; also some ginger syrup (see page 89) – or you could use the syrup from a jar of stem ginger. Naturally, Chinese cooks use their familiar long mooli, but our turnips work just fine, too. And I experimented with both!

Serves 4

600g turnips, peeled
250ml water
1 heaped tsp Maldon salt
10g dried porcini mushrooms
6 spring onions, trimmed
1 large green chilli, de-seeded (for less heat) if preferred
1 large red chilli, de-seeded (for less heat) if preferred
2 garlic cloves, peeled
100g tinned water chestnuts, drained
30g fresh ginger, peeled and finely grated
2 tsp sesame paste (see page 169)
1 tbsp ginger syrup (see page 89)
50ml Chinese rice wine
120g rice flour (an Oriental brand, if possible, but not the glutinous variety)
2–3 tbsp sesame oil

to serve

soy sauce
coriander sprigs

First grate the turnips (a food processor is the easiest way). Place in a pan, add the water and salt and stir together. Bring to a simmer, cover and cook for about 30 minutes, or until the grated turnip is very tender indeed – almost a mushy consistency.

Tip the turnips and liquor into a sieve set over a bowl and press down on the turnip using the back of a ladle to extract as much flavour and juice as possible. Drop the porcini mushrooms into this liquor and leave to soak for about 15 minutes until soft. In the meantime, finely chop the spring onions, chillies, garlic and water chestnuts (pulse in a small food processor for convenience).

Once soft, drain the porcini, reserving the liquor, and chop finely. Tip into a bowl and add the chopped ingredients, ginger, sesame paste and ginger syrup. Mix together well.

Pour the rice wine into a measuring jug and add 200ml of the reserved turnip/porcini liquor. Whisk the rice flour into this and then stir in the vegetable mixture.

Grease a small rectangular container (a small loaf tin or Tupperware box) with the sesame oil. Spoon in the turnip mixture, spreading it evenly. Cover with foil and put into a steamer. Steam over simmering water for 1½ hours, or until set and firm to the touch.

Take the container out of the steamer and remove the foil. After about 15 minutes, press a sheet of cling film over the surface of the turnip paste. Allow to cool completely and then chill in the fridge for at least 3–4 hours or, even better, overnight.

Remove from the fridge and run a little hot water onto the sides of the mould to loosen the cake. Turn the turnip cake out onto a chopping board and cut into slices, about 1.5cm thick, using a sharp knife dipped into a jug of boiled water.

Run a little sesame oil into a non-stick frying pan and place over a medium heat. Lay the slices in the pan and fry on both sides until a rich, dark brown colour; I like a few burnt spots, too. Place on a heated serving platter, dribble over some soy sauce and add the coriander sprigs.

Courgettes & Marrow

When I had access to my neighbour (and landlord) Tessa's courgettes for the entire summer, in that hot, hot and dry year of 1976, they became one of the daily vegetables for my little restaurant, on the Pembrokeshire coast.

The courgettes seemed almost inexhaustible and I was happily able to cut the evening's supply at about 6.30pm, every single day. I vaguely recall that Tessa charged me 5p per pound – and there were a few yellow ones, too, which really shocked some of my Welsh guests, who had never seen such a thing!

Come to think about it, I would not have been surprised if many of them had never seen a green one, either. In the mid-seventies, in Fishguard, finding something as simple as a tube of tomato purée was an adventure in itself. 'We've got ketchup, bach, will that do?' being a common answer to the weary question.

Not really knowing, then, at the relatively tender age of 22 years, quite how many diverse dishes I could muster with my bounty, I simply boiled thick slices of them for a minute or two in fiercely boiling, salted water, for each table, to order, then drained them and added a large knob of butter, together with a healthy grind of pepper. And, you know, those courgettes truly didn't need anything more than that.

Considering the first table's serving had still been on the plant only 45 minutes before, the taste of them was astonishingly fine and fresh. In fact, the customers often asked for seconds and I cheerfully complied: free food, happy diner.

However hard I tried to keep a track on the fast growth of my little patch, there would always suddenly appear, almost surreptitiously, a huge, lurking marrow beneath the giant leaves. Knowing perfectly well that this would not be the last time this oversight occurred, I would store it and wait patiently for the next discovery, thereby having enough to prepare my mother's deliciously bland recipe for 'marrow in white sauce', to serve with tasty roast legs of fabulous Welsh lamb for a traditional Sunday lunch.

I know that friends of mine don't see the point of marrow at all – and, in particular, the younger cooks of today, who seem only able to veer towards dishes that must offer intense flavours and exciting textures. Well, be that as it may. When carefully steamed chunks of tender, pale green marrow – and it is, to be sure, the most beautiful, pale green – are judiciously covered with a fine welter of smooth, white sauce scented with bay, clove and nutmeg, it is a dish of great class.

And, furthermore, if then baked in the oven with a sprinkling of grated cheese (Lancashire is good), it becomes one that is fit for a king.

Piquant courgettes with soured cream & dill

Although the paprika here is only used as a garnish at the end, it must be of good quality and freshly purchased. A good Hungarian brand would be ideal, otherwise use Spanish pimenton, but preferably not the very smoky variety.

Serves 2

700g–800g large courgettes, trimmed and coarsely grated
salt
25g butter
1 onion, peeled and thinly sliced
freshly ground white pepper
75g pickled dill cucumbers (preferably a Polish brand, such as Krakus)
2 tsp white wine vinegar
1 tbsp chopped dill, plus extra to garnish
4 tbsp soured cream
1 tsp caster sugar
a sprinkling of paprika, for garnish

Sprinkle the grated courgettes with salt only to season them, not more. Put them to drain in a colander with a dish underneath. Leave for 1 hour, then, using your hands, squeeze out the excess liquid. Put the courgettes to one side.

Melt the butter in a heavy-based cooking pot. Add the onion and stew until soft, but not coloured. Tip in the courgettes and stir them around with the onions until well mixed. Grind over a little pepper, put on the lid and cook very gently for about 5–7 minutes, stirring occasionally.

Using a blender, purée the dill cucumbers with the vinegar, dill and sugar.

Remove the lid from the courgettes, turn up the heat and, if necessary, drive off any excess liquid. Add the purée, stir in the soured cream and bring the mixture up to a simmer. Cook for a few more minutes until the assembly is thick and unctuous. Check for seasoning.

Turn into a heated serving dish or divide between individual shallow soup bowls. Sprinkle with extra chopped dill and generously sprinkle with paprika. A comforting and sloppy dish for Sunday supper, perhaps topped with a poached egg.

Courgette timbale with pimento dressing

If I may humbly say, a carefully considered vegetarian option.

Serves 4

- 500g courgettes, trimmed and coarsely grated
- 1 tsp salt
- 25g butter
- freshly ground white pepper
- 2 large eggs
- 1 large egg yolk
- 200g crème fraîche
- 2 heaped tsp finely grated Parmesan
- 2 tsp finely chopped dill
- 2 tsp finely snipped chives
- the merest scrap of garlic, crushed and finely chopped
- a little softened butter

for the pimento dressing

- 1 small garlic clove, peeled and finely chopped
- salt and freshly ground pepper
- 1 tsp sherry vinegar
- 1 tsp Dijon mustard
- 5 tbsp good olive oil
- 1 tbsp boiling water
- few shakes of Tabasco
- 75g roasted peppers (from a jar), finely chopped

Mix the grated courgettes with the salt, put to drain in a colander and leave for 1 hour. Squeeze thoroughly dry in a tea towel.

Preheat the oven to 150°C/gas mark 2. Melt the butter in a roomy frying pan and add the courgettes with some pepper. Cook gently for 10 minutes or so. Allow them to lightly gild, but also try to make sure that any excess moisture produced is driven off by the heat. Tip onto a plate to cool.

Put the eggs, egg yolk, crème fraîche, Parmesan, herbs and garlic into a roomy bowl and mix to combine, but do not over-beat; if this 'custard' is too light and airy, it will puff too much while cooking and then, unattractively, sink back. Stir the cooled courgettes into the custard and rectify the seasoning.

Generously butter 4 ramekins, place a tiny circle of greaseproof paper in the bottom of each and fill to the brim with the mixture. Stand them in a deep roasting tin and add boiling water to come at least two-thirds of the way up the sides of the ramekins. Bake for about 30 minutes, or until just firm to the touch.

Meanwhile, prepare the dressing. Whisk the garlic, seasoning and vinegar together in a bowl to dissolve the salt. Now whisk in the mustard, oil, water and Tabasco. Finally, stir in the roasted peppers.

Remove the ramekins from the water bath and leave to cool slightly for 10 minutes. Run a small, sharp knife around the edges of the custards and then carefully turn out onto serving plates. Pour the sauce over or around to suit yourself. Best eaten warm.

Marrow & tomato masala

This wonderfully aromatic dish is unusually delicious. Marrow, being the bland but texturally soothing vegetable it is, throws out much liquid as it cooks. Here, together with juices from the tomatoes – as they pop and burst in the heat of the assembly – it produces a dish that would not seem out of place on a stall in the streets of Mumbai, perhaps ladled out of some giant, tin cauldron. In fact, so copious are the juices generated here, it is almost a chunky broth.

If you don't fancy eating the skin of the marrow, simply scoop off the flesh with a spoon and leave the skin behind. However, if the marrow is fresh and young, this should not be necessary. Do try and find curry leaves, however, as they do add to the aroma of the thing.

Serves 4

1 marrow, about 1 kg
salt
2 onions, peeled and thinly sliced
2 garlic cloves, peeled and sliced
2 tbsp vegetable oil
1 tbsp masala paste (see page 52)
about 12 curry leaves, fresh or dried (optional)
750g ripe, red cherry, or baby plum tomatoes
50g butter, thinly sliced
freshly ground pepper

Preheat the oven to 160°C/gas mark 3. Trim the ends of the marrow, cut it in half down through the middle and then halve each piece lengthways. Scrape out the fibre and seeds with a teaspoon and then cut each quarter in half yet again, also lengthways, giving 8 marrow 'boats'.

Sprinkle salt generously over all cut surfaces and place the marrow in a colander for about 40 minutes to leach out a modicum of the juices. Rinse and dry in a tea towel.

Meanwhile, in a large, lidded pot, fry the onions and garlic in the oil until golden. Add the masala paste and stir around for a few minutes. Lay the marrow pieces, skin side down, on top and add the curry leaves, if using, then tip over the tomatoes. Season and dot with the slices of butter. Cover and place in the oven to cook for about 1½ hours.

Delicately decant into deep soup plates, so each one has two pieces of marrow, a spoonful of the tomatoes and plenty of aromatic broth.

Mushrooms Tame & Wild

Although I think I may have made mention of this before, it seems that the common or garden button mushroom has all but disappeared from the menu of most British restaurants. It is almost as if the chef doesn't think it quite good enough, an embarrassment to his good taste and exotic sensibilities.

Well, I can only see this as a great shame, for there is nothing nicer, as far as I am concerned than, say, a summery dish of diminutive button mushrooms cooked à la Grecque, or a trio of large and dark, open-cap fellows baked en persillade with a golden, breadcrumbed crust. And then, of course, there is a simple, smooth-as-silk cream of mushroom soup garnished with tiny, buttery croûtons – and also very good served chilled, in summer.

No, these days, it seems that all mushroom dishes, or those that include them, must be wild, or at least dried wild, or cultivated fungi such as shitake, oyster and those miniature, spooky and string-like enoki (flammulina velutipes, as I'm sure you know), which are a particular favourite of the cook who thinks he or she is inclined towards the Asian school. And, ironically, it is the regular use of these wild and faux-wild fungi on restaurant menus that partly contributed towards the title of this book.

Alongside goat's cheese, sun-dried (or oven-roasted) tomatoes, rocket and, occasionally, aubergines, it is to the wild mushroom that chefs prefer to turn when faced with the 'vegetarian option' for that day's lunch menu. I also reckon that this task is often given to the lowliest chef de partie in the kitchen, as the other cooks are far too busy getting ready to 'froth' and 'foam' all kinds of sauce and emulsion.

Ergo, it is out with the pasta or rice, and into a bowl of warm water with a handful of wrinkly dried fungi. That is not to say that the resultant dish might not be quite delicious, but I never understand why someone does not, just occasionally, cook some sliced button mushrooms with shallots, dry vermouth, a little cream and, say, some chopped tarragon, then pile them onto a slice of buttered toast or, even better, onto a slice of crisp, fried bread. Serve with a simple green salad and there is as delicious an option as I can think of. But there are always exceptions: fresh morels cooked in cream, for instance.

If you are lucky enough to either forage fresh native morels in the spring, or find a greengrocer or food hall that will stock them, then this is something special indeed. For best results, I find it quite unnecessary to fry them first, though most chefs will. Rather, after first rinsing and drying them in a tea towel, I add them directly to a pan with a clove of garlic crushed to a paste with salt, some pepper and a small knob of butter, then pour on enough whipping cream just to cover them. I let them stew gently until the cream has noticeably thickened, the morels softening but retaining a pleasing sponginess (taste one), then stir in a spoonful of snipped chives and a squeeze of lemon juice.

Eat this just as it is, or on toast or, if very hungry, stirred into some freshly cooked pasta. The rare wild mushroom not, for once, just an option, but the absolute reason for eating astonishingly good food.

Persillade of ceps & potatoes

There is something especially aromatic and magical that occurs when parsley and garlic are finely hand chopped together. Apart from anything else, the smell is intoxicating, as the juices mingle together under the blows from a heavy blade. I promise you that the end result, once heat is applied, is not quite the same if the two have been prepared separately.

Serves 2

2 medium, waxy potatoes, peeled
4–6 medium to large ceps (fresh or frozen), cleaned
large handful of flat parsley leaves
2 garlic cloves, peeled and lightly crushed
3–4 tbsp olive oil
salt and freshly ground pepper

Finely shred the potatoes (the shredder attachment of a food processor is ideal), then wash under cold running water until the water is clear. Drain and dry well in a tea towel. Thinly slice the ceps. Finely chop the parsley and garlic together.

Heat 2 tbsp of the olive oil in a large frying pan (preferably non-stick) and quickly fry the ceps with a little seasoning, until lightly coloured. Remove to a plate with a slotted spoon. Add another 1 tbsp oil to the pan and sauté the potatoes with a little seasoning until beginning to colour. Re-introduce the ceps and mingle with the parsley and garlic. Toss together over a brisk heat until smelling quite wonderful. Eat without delay.

Mushroom salad with Parmesan vinaigrette

As simple and savoury as can be, and all the better for that.

Serves 2
300g firm, white button
or closed cup mushrooms
juice of ½ lemon
scant 1 tbsp white wine vinegar
2 tbsp hand-hot water
salt and freshly ground white pepper
1 very small garlic clove, peeled and crushed
1–2 tbsp freshly grated Parmesan
2–3 tbsp extra virgin olive oil
2 tbsp whipping cream
1 very small shallot, peeled and finely chopped
plenty of freshly chopped parsley

Thinly slice the mushrooms and place in a shallow dish suitable for serving. Squeeze over the lemon juice and stir together. Put to one side.

Whiz the vinegar, water and seasoning together in a small food processor for a second or two to dissolve the salt, then introduce the garlic, 1 tbsp of the Parmesan and the olive oil. Blend to homogenise the mixture, then add the cream and give a final quick whiz; do not over-process at this stage for fear of curdling the cream.

Pour the dressing over the mushrooms, gently mix together and then neaten the arrangement for serving. Finally, sprinkle over the shallot, parsley and remaining Parmesan, to taste. Eat with slices of warm and buttered, crusty baguette.

Mushroom consomme

Delicious supped with Rachel Cooke's wonderful Parmesan biscuits (see page 214) alongside, but perhaps cut into fingers, rather than rounds, so more closely resembling a cheese sablé.

Note that if you are serving the consommé hot, you may like to add a further splash of Madeira. Or if serving cold, carefully float a spoonful or two of lightly whipped whipping cream – flavoured with some finely chopped tarragon leaves and scantily acidulated with tarragon vinegar – upon the surface of the consommé.

Serves 4

- 2 large onions, about 350g, peeled and thickly sliced
- 3–4 tbsp olive oil
- 750g flat, dark-gilled mushrooms, thinly sliced
- 3 garlic cloves, peeled and crushed
- salt and freshly ground pepper
- 125ml dry vermouth
- 1 ½ litres stock

for the clarification

- 250g flat, dark-gilled mushrooms, sliced
- 100g celery, chopped
- 3 or 4 tarragon sprigs
- 1 tbsp tarragon vinegar
- 3 large egg whites
- 100ml Madeira

Using a large pot, very slowly fry the onions in 2–3 tbsp of the olive oil until a rich, golden brown colour; this will take 30 minutes or so. Remove with a slotted spoon to a plate and reserve.

Put the mushrooms in the pot, now, with a little more oil if necessary and also cook until golden brown. Add the garlic and seasoning, turn up the heat and stir-fry for a couple of minutes. Add the vermouth and allow to bubble vigorously. Reintroduce the reserved, cooked onions and then pour in the stock. Cover and simmer gently for 40 minutes. Strain the broth into a clean pan, leave to settle and then remove any fat with sheets of kitchen paper, briefly laid upon the surface. Allow to cool.

For the clarification, whiz together all the ingredients in a food processor until smooth-ish. Whisk the mixture into the mushroom broth and slowly bring up to a simmer, stirring until it is becoming quite hot. Now leave the broth to gently bubble under what will be a raft of mushroom mush, floating on the surface; check that this is fully floating, as you do not wish for any solids sitting on the base of the pan, which will burn. Allow the liquor to continue blipping its way through the raft for about 30 minutes.

Strain the broth through a strainer lined with a double-folded sheet of muslin or a fine, linen tea towel. Leave to drip through this to reveal – hopefully – a crystal clear consommé beneath. Serve hot, or chilled in summertime.

Gratin of stuffed mushrooms

Serves 4

- 8 large flat mushrooms, with deep interiors for stuffing
- 50g butter
- 1 onion, peeled and finely chopped
- 1 large celery stick, peeled and finely chopped
- salt and freshly ground pepper
- grated zest and juice of 1 large lemon
- 75g fresh white breadcrumbs
- 2 hard-boiled eggs, grated
- 2 tbsp chopped parsley
- 1 tsp thyme leaves
- 2 garlic cloves, peeled and finely chopped
- 2 tbsp olive oil
- 8 tbsp double cream
- 1–2 tbsp freshly grated Gruyère
- lemon wedges, to serve (optional)

Preheat the oven to 180°C/gas mark 4. Remove the stalks from the mushrooms and set the caps to one side; finely chop the stalks.

Melt the butter in a deep frying pan and fry the onion, celery and chopped mushroom stalks with a little salt and pepper until pale golden. Tip into a bowl and add the lemon zest, breadcrumbs, eggs, parsley, thyme and garlic. Mix thoroughly with a fork and try not to compact the mix. Put to one side.

Heat the olive oil in a solid-based baking dish – one that will happily transfer from stove top to oven. Slide in the mushroom caps, open side down; they should fit snugly. Lightly season and allow the mushrooms to gently sizzle before turning them over. Remove from the heat and squeeze over the lemon juice.

Now fill each mushroom cap with some of the stuffing mixture, but do not pat it down. Bake in the oven for 25–30 minutes, turning the oven down slightly if the stuffing is browning too much.

Turn the oven setting up to 200°C, gas mark 6. Using a small knife, check to see that the mushrooms are tender, then pour a spoonful of cream over each one. Lightly sprinkle with the Gruyère and return to the top shelf of the oven. Continue to cook until the cream is bubbling and the cheese lightly gilded.

Serve the mushrooms at once, with extra lemon squeezed over if desired. Delicious eaten with a simply dressed watercress salad.

HERBS

Parsley, Sage, Rosemary & Thyme

The one particular failure of living in a first floor flat in West London is that of enough space to grow herbs. I guess I wouldn't really want a garden unless it was in the countryside, but enough essential herbs growing seasonally all year round would be a veritable boon.

I would like a bushy bay tree, for one. Similarly, a rosemary bush. Hardy thymes, too, and sage, of course. Then I could indulge in masses of basil, one or two varieties of mint, both types of parsley, chives and the deliciously delicate chervil. Tarragon (the French, obviously, rather than the tasteless impostor, the weed-like Russian) would be at the top of the list, too. Oh that I could!

I have an outdoor windowsill that will accommodate a couple of boxes, which I am happy to fill with favourites during the summer: garden mint, mainly, and some basil plants for the shorter, hotter periods. But that is it, really. Parsley might just be there, too, but one recipe demanding a big presence would surely decimate its short life in one cutting. I adore lots of parsley around me, so am resigned to purchase.

Bay, I filch with permission, from Father Huw Chiplin, my local vicar, who has a convenient front garden to his vicarage, which I regularly pass on my way to the corner shop. There he has four – four! – healthy bay trees behind his wall and, armed with my trusty kitchen scissors, I snip, snip, snip my way along his bushes, fussily, only collecting the largest branches with the largest leaves. These I then dry in the kitchen and thank The Lord, and his employee, for such generous gifts. Huw's bushes really are particularly fragrant, I must say, and easily comparable with some filched leaves (without permission, I am now embarrassed to say) from a side street in sunny Beaulieu, in the South of France on another occasion.

These days, fresh herbs are vital to my cooking, but it was not always the case. It is now so very easy to forget a time when such luxuries – and yes, they are, don't forget – were simply an unthinkable asset to the kitchen of the keen, home cook. Moreover, even during my apprenticeship in a French restaurant in the North of England, an occasional bunch of fresh tarragon in a brown paper bag would travel up to Manchester by train from London, tucked amongst other essentials: dried wild mushrooms (morels, ceps, girolles), Bayonne ham, preserved truffles and walnut oil.

Very occasionally, a few of these fresh leaves would be chopped up to further enhance a béarnaise sauce, then scented with a reduction involving some powdery dried leaves, though as fine as these could be. But, generally, the entire leafy offering would be plunged into a large jar of vinegar to, ironically, then flavour it for use in a reduction for – you've guessed it – more béarnaise sauce. Hey ho!

For once, we really must thank the supermarkets – and greengrocers and farmers' markets – for their abundance of fresh herbs, to enhance our cooking each and every day. Remember, once upon a time, the only parsley one might come home with – freely, granted – was a few sprigs wrapped up with a pound of Friday cod fillet.

Parsley, radish & celery salad with capers

Simple, fragrant, sharp and crisp. Make sure that all the salad ingredients are cold before assembly.

Serves 2

small bunch of flat-leaf parsley, leaves only, roughly torn
7–8 long French radishes, trimmed and quartered
1 shallot, peeled and very finely sliced into rings
3 small celery sticks, taken from the heart, cut into batons
2 tsp capers, together with 2 tsp of their vinegar
squeeze of lemon juice
salt and freshly ground pepper
2 tbsp extra virgin olive oil

Mix everything together in a large bowl and turn out onto a serving dish. Eat with buttered slices of warmed baguette.

Butter beans with sage, olive oil & dried chilli

If you prefer an even spicier flavour, you might like to use half olive oil and half chilli oil.

Serves 4, generously
300g dried butter beans
750ml water or stock
1 whole head of garlic, sliced in half across its middle
3–4 sage sprigs
3–4 small, dried red chillies
4–5 tbsp olive oil
salt

Put the beans into a large saucepan, cover with plenty of water (not the given amount) and bring up to the boil. Switch off the heat, cover and leave for 1 hour. Drain and rinse in a colander under cold running water.

Preheat the oven to 160°C/gas mark 3. Put the beans into a lidded, solid pot and cover with the 750ml water or stock. Slowly bring to a simmer and skim off any scum that forms on the surface. Add all the other ingredients except the salt and stir. Put on the lid and bake in the oven for about 1 hour, until the beans are tender. Only now add salt to taste; added at the beginning of the cooking process it will toughen the skins.

Ladle into shallow soup plates and serve warm, rather than piping hot.

A sprinkling of fine vinegar would make the beans even nicer, for me.

Roasted shallots with rosemary

I am loathe to suggest adding salt to this recipe, as once the stock used has reduced, there should be enough. You can always add a touch more at the end, if necessary.

Serves 4
2 tbsp olive oil
25g butter
24 large shallots, peeled (not the extra large 'banana' shallots)
scant sprinkling of sugar
freshly ground white pepper
4 tbsp white wine vinegar
100ml stock
several bushy rosemary sprigs

Preheat the oven to 190°C/gas mark 5. Heat the olive oil and butter in a solid and shallow, stove-top-to-oven casserole (a Le Creuset would be ideal, here). Once hot, add the shallots and gently fry, turning them regularly, until lightly coloured all over. Sprinkle with the sugar and pepper and pour in the wine vinegar. Allow the vinegar to bubble away to almost nothing and then pour in the stock.

Bring up to the boil, tuck in the rosemary sprigs and put into the oven. Bake for 40 minutes or so, turning the shallots over once, until soft, well burnished and the stock has reduced to a sticky juice. Serve directly from the dish.

Thyme, onion & Gruyère tart

Very savoury indeed and so lovely and fondant, too.

Serves 4–6

for the pastry

65g cold butter, cut into cubes
100g plain flour
pinch of salt
1–2 tbsp iced water

for the filling

50g butter
750g white onions, peeled and very thinly sliced
1 large egg
2 large egg yolks
200ml double cream
2 tsp Dijon mustard
1 tsp thyme leaves
salt and freshly ground white pepper
60g Gruyère, freshly grated
freshly grated nutmeg

To make the pastry, briefly process the butter, flour and salt together in a food processor until the mixture resembles fine breadcrumbs. Now tip into a large, roomy bowl and gently mix in the water with cool hands or a table knife, until well amalgamated. Knead the dough lightly, then put into a plastic bag and chill in the fridge for at least 1 hour before rolling.

For the filling, melt the butter in a wide, shallow pan. Tip in the onions and very gently sweat over a moderate heat for at least 40 minutes, or as long as 1 hour, until pale golden and completely soft. Cool.

Meanwhile, preheat the oven to 180°C/gas mark 4, and place a flat baking sheet inside to heat (it will help the base of the tart to cook thoroughly).

Roll out the pastry on a lightly floured surface as thinly as you dare, then use to line a 20cm tart tin, 3cm deep. Prick the base with a fork. Line the pastry case with foil and dried beans, slide onto the hot baking sheet and bake 'blind' for about 15–20 minutes. Remove the foil and beans and return the pastry case to the oven for a further 10 minutes or so, until it is golden, crisp and well cooked through, particularly the base.

Mix together the egg, egg yolks, cream, mustard and thyme leaves. Carefully mix in the onions, season and pile the mixture into the pastry case. Sprinkle the Gruyère over the surface and generously grate over some nutmeg. Bake in the oven for about 45 minutes, or until the filling is a rich golden colour and just firm to the touch. Leave to stand for 10 minutes before eating.

Potato pancakes with soured cream & chives

To make clarified butter, melt a packet of unsalted butter in a small pan until there is froth on the surface and a milky residue on the bottom. Remove the froth with a spoon and discard, then ladle out the clear butter into a container, leaving the milky residue behind. You will not need all the clarified butter here, but it keeps well in the fridge, covered, for a few weeks. The milky residue can be used in the pancake batter – top up with milk to give the 50ml required. Waste not want not, I always say.

Serves 4

for the pancake batter

- 500g potatoes, peeled and cut into large chunks
- 50ml milk
- 2½ tbsp plain flour
- 3 large eggs
- 4 large egg whites
- 2 ½ tbsp double cream
- salt and freshly ground pepper
- clarified butter for frying

for the soured cream and chives

- 150ml soured cream
- 2 tbsp snipped chives
- large pinch of cayenne pepper
- pinch of salt

Warm the oven to low in advance and put a large ovenproof plate inside to warm up. Steam the potatoes until cooked, or boil carefully and allow to dry out in the warm oven. While still hot, put through a mouli-légumes or a potato ricer; do not use a food processor or the potato will become gluey. Allow to cool slightly in a mixing bowl. Now beat in the milk, flour, eggs, egg whites, cream and seasoning.

For the soured cream and chives, mix everything together in a bowl and adjust the seasoning if you need to.

Heat a little of the clarified butter in a heavy-based frying pan or on a cast-iron flat griddle pan. You will need to cook the pancakes in batches: pour 3 or 4 small ladlefuls of the batter onto the surface of the pan, spacing them apart. Moderate to high heat is called for here; you need a slight sizzle and a light browning at the edges of the pancake after about 2 minutes.

The time to turn over is when the tiniest bubbles appear on the uncooked surface. Take a palette knife and quickly flip the pancake over. The cooked surface should be perfectly mottled with pale brown blisters and have a thin golden ring around the edge.

Finish cooking for a further minute or so. The texture should be slightly springy but feel moist. As you cook the pancakes, keep them warm in the oven on the plate, covered with foil.

Hand round the pancakes and the soured cream and chives separately, so that each person may pop a dollop onto each pancake. Very delicious.

Chilled curried mint & cucumber soup

Another way one can fashion this soup is to reduce the curry powder to 1–2 tsp. Once the soup has cooled to tepid, whisk in 2 tbsp of the lovely green paste (below), or to taste. Even more delicious…

Serves 4

1 large cucumber
salt and freshly ground white pepper
25g butter
1 small onion, peeled and chopped
1 tbsp curry powder
200ml stock
1 small sweet apple, peeled, cored and chopped
150ml plain yoghurt
150ml coconut milk
75ml whipping cream
2 tbsp chopped mint
juice of 1 small lime
1 small, hot green chilli, de-seeded and chopped (optional)

Peel the cucumber, cut in half lengthways and scoop the seeds out, using a teaspoon; reserve the skin and seeds. Finely dice the cucumber flesh, mix with a little salt and place in a colander to drain for 30 minutes or so.

Meanwhile, melt the butter in a saucepan and fry the onion until soft. Stir in the curry powder and cook together for a few more minutes, then add the stock and diced apple. Simmer for about 20 minutes or until the apple is very tender. Cool.

Once cooled, purée the soup with the yoghurt, coconut milk and the reserved cucumber debris (seeds, skins, etc.) using a blender until very smooth indeed. Pass through a fine sieve into a bowl and then stir in the cream. Season with salt and pepper to taste.

Briefly rinse the diced cucumber and squeeze lightly to remove excess liquid. Stir into the soup with the mint, lime juice and, if liked, the green chilli. Cover and chill in the fridge for at least 2 hours before serving, in chilled soup bowls.

Green paste

This wonderful, spicy and fragrant condiment is utilised in other recipes in the book, such as the samosas (on page 64). Store it in the fridge and its colour will remain green for 2 or 3 days, or pack into small, lidded plastic pots and freeze – to keep it fresh and verdant for longer.

To fill 2 small pots

7–10 hot or mild green chillies, to taste
90g coriander leaves
40g mint leaves
8 garlic cloves, peeled and crushed
2 tsp ground cumin
1 tsp sugar
1 heaped tsp sea salt
75ml lime juice
100g creamed coconut (from a block), coarsely grated

De-seed the chillies or not, depending on your heat threshold. Place in a small food processor together with all the other ingredients and whiz to make a smooth purée. Scrape out into a lidded plastic container and put into the fridge.

Soupe au pistou

Nice in Nice and nice anywhere, anyway.

Serves 6

200g leeks, trimmed, thinly sliced and washed
100g celery, peeled and chopped
2 tbsp olive oil
200g potatoes, peeled and diced
150g aubergine, peeled and diced
200g courgettes, trimmed and diced
1.25–1.5 litres water
2 tsp Maldon salt
250g spring greens, or other green cabbage, chopped
150g spinach or chard leaves, washed and chopped
50g spaghetti, broken into short lengths
100g French beans, topped, tailed and cut into 2cm lengths
1 x 400g tin haricot beans, drained and rinsed
freshly ground white pepper

for the pistou

100ml extra virgin olive oil
large bunch of basil
3 garlic cloves, peeled and crushed
3 tbsp freshly grated pecorino or Parmesan cheese

In a large pan or cooking pot, gently stew the leeks and celery in the olive oil until softened. Tip in the potatoes, aubergine and courgettes, then pour in the water and add the salt. Bring up to a simmer and cook for 10 minutes.

Now stir in the spring greens, spinach and spaghetti. Cook for a further 10 minutes, then stir in the French beans, haricot beans and pepper. Bring the soup up to a final, gentle simmer and continue cooking for a further 20–30 minutes, or until all is very soft, thick and a nice dull-ish green colour – as it should be.

For the pistou, simply purée all the ingredients together using a small food processor; or, if you are an artisan pistou maker, employ a pestle and mortar.

I like to eat this soup almost at room temperature, or at least warm rather than piping hot, with the pistou handed round separately, so that each person can add as little or as much as they like.

PASTA

Macaroni & Cannelloni

Unlike many of my peers, when I was still cooking in a restaurant kitchen, the fabrication of home-made pasta was never very high on my list of special food. As near perfect pastry as we could achieve, yes. The smoothest and most freshly churned ice creams and sorbets, yes. The highest risen, crisp-and-yet-soft-inside and cooked to order Yorkshire puddings for Sunday lunch, most definitely. But rolling out sheets of fresh pasta, well, no, not really. Nothing against it at all, it is just that I think there are other cooks – Italians, obviously – who, quite simply, make it much better. They have an affinity with it. The making of pasta is in their blood.

Since leaving the professional role I now do, occasionally, enjoy dusting off the pasta machine to roll out lovely thin sheets of yellow pasta for the making of ravioli – as you will realise from the butternut squash ravioli (on page 38), which are very simply formed. There is no stamping out with little fluted cutters or some such, they are simply folded over into raggedy little square-ish packages. For me, the most important part of the operation is to take the pasta to the machine's final setting (ratchet 7, on mine), so achieving the ultimate, delicate wrapper. This will also help when pressing together the edges of the ravioli, which are, in effect, double the thickness, now, and must be squeezed between the fingertips to make them as thin as possible. Failure to do this can result in a tough and doughy edge.

Personally, if cooking regular pasta at home – spaghetti, tagliatelle, linguine, that kind of thing – I will always prefer to use a fine quality dried brand. Cipriani egg pasta is my particular favourite and usually carries the additional qualification of being 'extra sotilli': extra thin. It is a beautiful product, priced accordingly but never disappoints. If you cannot find Cipriani pasta (it is mostly available in speciality food shops, Italian delis and, occasionally, supermarkets), then I would recommend De Cecco.

One of the most gorgeous pasta dishes of my life is the one that Franco Taruschio used to make when he and his wife, Ann, were at The Walnut Tree, near Abergavenny, in Wales. The dish was called Vincisgrassi and involved alternating layers of lasagne, sliced porcini, thin slices of prosciutto crudo, béchamel and Parmesan. And if truffles were in season, these would further be shaved over each piping hot – and I mean, piping – serving, just after emerging from the oven.

I have successfully made a vegetarian version of this wonderful dish by, obviously, leaving out the ham and, instead, substituting briefly cooked spinach, refreshed in iced water, squeezed of excess moisture and then distributed as a pretty green strata between the pasta and porcini. If porcini are unavailable, then sliced flat mushrooms are a most serviceable alternative – if not with quite so heady an aroma.

Mushroom cannelloni

I know it seems odd that I have chosen to use a tin of Heinz tomato soup here, but I really like the flavour it gives to the sauce for this particular dish. My reasoning is that some time ago, for cannelloni, I used a carton of Spanish-made tomato sauce, which was very smooth and thick, but also had a flavour similar to the Heinz soup. All who tasted it thought it was terrific – and had no idea it had come from a carton. As the Spanish sauce is not available to all, this method attempts to replicate it.

Serves 4

for the thick tomato sauce

2 garlic cloves, peeled and crushed
50g butter, plus a little extra, softened, to butter the dish
2 x 400g tins chopped tomatoes
salt
1 x 300g tin Heinz tomato soup

for the cannelloni filling

1 onion, peeled and chopped
2 garlic cloves, peeled and chopped
30g butter
200g flat mushrooms, roughly chopped
salt and freshly ground pepper
2–3 tarragon sprigs, leaves only, chopped
2–3 parsley sprigs, leaves only, chopped
juice of ½ lemon
big splash of dry vermouth

for the béchamel sauce

500ml milk
1 bay leaf
freshly grated nutmeg
60g butter
35g plain flour

to assemble

8 cannelloni tubes (De Cecco brand, for preference)
2–3 heaped tbsp freshly grated Parmesan

Lightly butter a large, shallow, ovenproof baking dish that will easily hold 8 cannelloni tubes, with space in between each one.

For the thick tomato sauce, in a saucepan, stew the garlic in the butter until pale golden. Add the tomatoes and very little salt. Gently simmer until reduced by almost two-thirds; the sauce should be very thick. Pass it through a sieve directly into the baking dish, spreading it around with a spoon until level. Put to one side.

For the cannelloni filling, fry the onion and garlic in the butter to soften. Add the mushrooms, season and stew until all is soft and fragrant. Add the herbs, lemon juice and vermouth, turn up the heat and cook until almost dry. Leave to cool, then whiz in a food processor until somewhere between coarse and fine. Preheat the oven to 180°C/gas mark 4.

To make the béchamel sauce, heat the milk with the bay, nutmeg and a little salt. Simmer for a few minutes, then cover and allow the flavours to mingle for 10 minutes. In another pan, melt the butter and stir in the flour. Cook gently for a minute or two to make a roux, but do not allow it to colour. Filch out the bay, add the milk and whisk vigorously until smooth. On the lowest possible heat (preferably using a heat-diffuser mat), set the sauce to cook for about 15–20 minutes, stirring fairly constantly, using a wooden spoon. The consistency will soon become silky and unctuous. Add pepper, check for salt, switch off the heat and cover with a tight-fitting lid; this helps to prevent a skin forming. Keep warm.

Once cooled, fully fill the cannelloni tubes with the mushroom mixture (I find a piping bag is the most efficient way). Lay them side by side in the dish, pushing them into the tomato sauce. Make sure all is neat and then blanket with the béchamel sauce. Shake the dish a little to settle everything and sprinkle the entire surface with Parmesan. Bake for

40–50 minutes until all is bubbling and well crusted.

Spaghetti al aglio & peperoncino

I love the way the sticky, golden garlic behaves when cooking with the chilli and oil. Heavenly smell, too!

Serves 2

6 garlic cloves, peeled and sliced
2 large red chillies, thinly sliced
4–5 tbsp extra virgin olive oil
200g dried spaghetti
salt

Cook the garlic and chillies very gently in a small pan with the olive oil, until the garlic is pale golden and both are crisp. Lift out with a slotted spoon and put onto a small plate; reserve the oil.

Cook the spaghetti in a large pan of salted boiling water until al dente. Drain well in a colander and rinse with warm water.

Now take a large frying pan (preferably non-stick) and add some of the flavoured oil. Heat gently and then tip in the spaghetti. Turn and toss the pasta around until well coated with oil. Add the chilli and garlic and toss until well dispersed.

Turn the spaghetti onto two very hot plates, adding a little extra oil if you think it necessary. Eat without delay.

Tagliatelle with runner beans, basil & mint

I like the mimicry here between the strands of pasta and the sliced runner beans.

Serves 4, as a light lunch or supper

- 450–500g runner beans, topped and tailed
- 25g butter
- 300ml whipping cream
- 150g soft cream cheese
- 1 large garlic clove, peeled and finely chopped
- ½ tsp Maldon salt
- freshly ground white pepper
- generous grating of nutmeg
- 40g Parmesan, freshly grated, plus extra for serving
- 175g Cipriani tagliatelle, or other fine quality egg tagliatelle
- 2 handfuls of basil leaves
- handful of mint leaves

Prepare the runner beans in the traditional way, slicing them lengthways, using a 'bean zip', thereby removing the outer stringy sides.

Put the butter, cream, cream cheese, garlic, seasoning, nutmeg and Parmesan into a medium pan and slowly bring to a simmer, gently whisking at the same time to melt everything together. Put to one side.

Have a large bowl of well-iced water ready. Add the beans to a large pan of generously salted boiling water and cook until just tender. Lift them out in batches with a large slotted spoon and immediately immerse them in the iced water, dispersing them with your hands to cool them down as swiftly as possible. Don't discard the cooking water.

Once the beans are really cold, tip them into a large colander and drain thoroughly. Return to the (now empty) bowl and stand it in the sink.

Now, making sure that there aren't any stray bits of cooked bean in the reserved cooking water, bring it back to the boil. Add the pasta and cook until al dente. Carefully balance the colander over the beans in the bowl and drain the pasta over them; this will, effectively, reheat the beans at the same time.

Lift out the colander, shaking out any clinging water from the draining pasta, and place on the draining board. Lift the bowl of beans in hot water out of the sink. Replace the pasta colander in the sink and drain the beans over the pasta. Toss and shake the beans and pasta together using a couple of large forks, or salad servers, until evenly combined.

Coarsely chop the basil and mint leaves together, stir them into the reserved cream mixture and warm through. Pour into the pan in which the pasta was boiled and then add the pasta and beans. Over a very gentle heat, carefully lift and turn them through the cream and herb mixture until well coated and hot.

Serve on warmed plates and hand freshly grated Parmesan at table.

Macaroni cheese with tomatoes

Self explanatory, really, when all is said and done.

Serves 2

400ml milk
1 bay leaf
freshly grated nutmeg
salt and freshly ground white pepper
40g butter
25g plain flour
100g mature Cheddar or tasty Lancashire cheese, grated
150g macaroni
4 small, ripe tomatoes, thinly sliced
1 tbsp freshly grated Parmesan

To make the cheese sauce, heat the milk with the bay, nutmeg and a little salt. Simmer for a few minutes, then take off the heat, cover and allow the flavours to mingle for 10 minutes. Preheat the oven to 180°C/gas mark 4.

In another pan, melt the butter and stir in the flour. Cook gently for a minute or two to make a roux, but on no account allow it to colour. Remove the bay leaf, add the milk to the roux and vigorously whisk together until smooth.

Set the sauce to cook on the lowest possible heat (preferably using a heat-diffuser mat) and stir, fairly constantly, using a wooden spoon. The consistency will soon become silky and unctuous. After about 10–15 minutes, stir in the cheese, then add pepper and taste for salt. Cook for a further 3–4 minutes. Switch off the heat and cover with a tight-fitting lid; this helps to prevent a skin forming. Keep warm, nearby.

Add the macaroni to a pan of lightly salted boiling water and boil until tender, then drain very well. Mix with the cheese sauce and spoon into a lightly buttered baking dish. Cover with the tomatoes, slightly overlapping the slices, and sprinkle evenly with the Parmesan.

Bake in the oven for about 30–40 minutes, until the tomatoes are lightly blistered and the edges are bubbling up nicely, from underneath.

Gnocchi alla Romana

This may not be the most well known of gnocchi recipes, but it is a reassuringly comforting one. It is lovely eaten entirely on its own, or with tomato sauce (see page 21 or 158).

Serves 4, generously
1 litre milk
200g semolina
150g Parmesan, freshly grated
100g unsalted butter, cut into cubes
2 large egg yolks
1 rounded tsp Maldon salt
freshly ground white pepper
freshly grated nutmeg

In a roomy, heavy-bottomed pan, bring the milk up to the boil. Now, whisking constantly, pour in the semolina in a steady stream. Continue to whisk until it is thoroughly mixed in, without any lumps. Turn the heat to very low, exchange the whisk for a stout wooden spoon and continue cooking and stirring for a further 10 minutes, or so, until really thick.

Take off the heat and quickly beat in half the Parmesan and half the butter with the egg yolks, salt, pepper and nutmeg until well blended and smooth. Spray a flat baking tray lightly with water. Using a palette knife dipped into hot water, spread the mixture out evenly on the tray, to a thickness of 1–1.5cm. Leave to cool completely.

Preheat the oven to 220°C/gas mark 7. Lightly butter a large, oval baking dish. Using a 4cm pastry cutter, cut the cold paste into circles (a small dish of warm water to hand, in which to occasionally dip the cutter for a neat cut, is useful here).

Lay the gnocchi slightly overlapping in the baking dish, dot with the remaining butter and sprinkle with the rest of the cheese. Bake on an upper (but not top-most) shelf in the oven for about 15–20 minutes, until the gnocchi are nicely gilded and sizzling; a final quick flash under a grill can also be employed, if necessary.

Pappardelle with artichokes and sage

As simple and delicious as can be. If at all possible, use the Cipriani brand of pappardelle – packaged in a swish-looking, dark blue box – which is available online.

Serves 2
8 small artichokes
juice of 1 small lemon
2–3 tbsp extra virgin olive oil
2 garlic cloves, peeled and thinly sliced
6–7 sage leaves, roughly chopped
salt and freshly ground pepper
150g pappardelle
freshly grated Parmesan

Trim the outer leaves from the artichokes, slice off their tops and then slice thinly, discarding any choke. Immediately toss with the lemon juice.

In a non-stick frying pan, heat 2 tbsp of the olive oil and gently fry the artichokes until beginning to take on a pale golden colour. Add the garlic and sage and cook for a few more minutes until the garlic is lightly coloured, too. Season well and keep warm.

Cook the pappardelle in a large pan of lightly salted boiling water until al dente. Place a serving bowl in the sink and suspend a colander over it. Tip the pasta into the colander to drain; the boiling water will warm the bowl. Lift the colander, discard the water and tip the pasta into the bowl.

Toss the pasta with a little more olive oil. Add the artichokes and mix together. Serve on hot plates and hand round some Parmesan at table.

PULSES & GRAINS

Split Peas & Chick Peas

At the Diwana Bhel Poori House, behind London's Euston station, there is a daily vegetarian lunchtime buffet offered of such breadth, quality and value that I wonder why I don't venture there more often. There is almost every kind of pulse imaginable – assorted lentil dishes, sharply spiced and dressed bowls of chick peas, soupy dhals and various beans. Together with a colourful array of green vegetable dishes, potatoes and roots, it is, to be sure, a vegetarian heaven. Note, particularly, a dish piled high with dark green 'methi', the slightly bitter fenugreek leaf, so fragrantly delicious.

Here, in Britain, I feel we have never been interested enough in pulses to make of them anything more than sustenance. In the Northeast, there is the 'pease pudding', of course. To make it, typically, yellow split peas are cooked in stock until very soft indeed, beaten to a paste, an egg is added and then the mixture is either baked in the oven, or wrapped in muslin and boiled, until set firm. And as the nursery rhyme has it 'Pease Pudding Hot, Pease Pudding Cold...', either way, it is usually thickly sliced. I guess it is okay when served with the traditional ham it is often cooked with, but as a dish in its own right

– and with all due respect to the proud Geordie cook – well, I remain a touch unconvinced.

Most people's relationship with the chick pea now appears in the shape of a supermarket plastic pot of hummus. I don't decry this at all, being an occasional purchaser myself, but it bears no relationship whatsoever to the exquisitely fine pastes prepared in the kitchens of very good Lebanese and Middle Eastern restaurants, where a more correct amount – more generous, in fact – of tahini (sesame paste) is incorporated.

Even more importantly, for me, at least, is the amazing super-smooth consistency they manage to achieve. I am further captivated by its traditional presentation: in a small deep terracotta dish and smoothed up the sides to form a well, which is filled with good olive oil, a little cayenne/paprika and chopped parsley. Hot grilled pitta bread and lemons are the only accompaniments necessary. The hummus served at Al Waha, in Westbourne Grove, West London, is one of the very best I have eaten.

Greek fava

I first ate this when I was staying with some English friends in their house in the Peloponnese. It is very comforting and delicious when eaten spread onto toasted pitta bread. Although I think it is not traditional, I like to add garlic to the fava, too.

If you are able to find pale pink, mild and sweet-fleshed onions (often in Asian food stores) please use these.

Most would say that it is not necessary to soak split peas, these days. Well, not being most people, I do soak them; I find they cook more evenly and, as a result, turn out tender and soft.

Serves 2–3

150g yellow split peas, soaked overnight or for at least 6 hours in cold water
1 litre water
2 medium pink (or red) onions, peeled – 1 coarsely chopped; 1 finely sliced
4 garlic cloves, peeled and coarsely chopped
50ml extra virgin olive oil, plus a little extra to serve
salt and freshly ground pepper
1 lemon, quartered

Drain the soaked peas, place them in a cooking pot or heavy-bottomed pan and pour on the 1 litre water. Add the chopped onion, garlic and olive oil. Do not add any salt, for now. Bring up to the boil, skim off any scum that rises and simmer uncovered for about 1½ hours, adding salt only after the first hour. The peas must be very well cooked and turned almost to mush, without too much excess water; if necessary, drain some off.

Pass it all through the coarse blade of a vegetable mill (mouli-légumes), rather than use a food processor, which will purée the mixture too much.

Pour the fava into a warmed serving dish. Spoon over some more olive oil, scatter with the sliced onion and grind over plenty of pepper. Best eaten warm. Serve with cut lemons to squeeze over.

Simply dressed hearts of Cos lettuce would be an accompaniment with contrast, but I prefer to eat this just with toasted pitta.

Warm chick pea salad with sesame dressing

This salad is absolutely made by the inclusion of my sesame paste, which appears in several other recipes. Make sure the tinned chick peas are of good pedigree – ideally a Greek or Middle Eastern brand.

Serves 2

1 x 400–420g tin chick peas

for the dressing

2 tsp sesame seeds
2 ripe tomatoes
1 garlic clove, peeled and finely chopped
2 spring onions, trimmed and finely sliced
1 heaped tbsp black olives, chopped
2 tsp red wine vinegar
2 tbsp olive oil (from the olives if packed in oil)
1 tbsp sesame paste (see below)
1 tbsp each of freshly chopped, flat-leaf parsley and mint

For the dressing, lightly toast the sesame seeds in a dry pan over a medium heat until fragrant and cool slightly. Peel, de-seed and chop the tomatoes and mix together with the rest of the dressing ingredients in a roomy bowl.

Tip the chick peas into a pan, bring to a simmer and heat briefly for a few minutes. Drain in a sieve and rinse with boiled water from the kettle.

Add the hot chick peas to the dressing, stir together and serve, spooned over slices of toasted sourdough or country bread, if you like.

Sesame paste

You need a powerful, small food processor to make this paste. For the best flavour, I feel it is important to use Asian brands of chilli and sesame oils.

Makes about 400ml

100g sesame seeds
75g ginger, peeled and finely grated (juice saved!)
1 large garlic clove, peeled and crushed
2 tbsp light soy sauce
4 tbsp Japanese mirin
1–2 tbsp Asian chilli oil
100–125ml Asian sesame oil, plus a little extra to serve
2 tbsp lemon juice
125ml warm water
1–2 tbsp sugar, to taste

Lightly toast the sesame seeds in a dry pan over a medium heat until fragrant and cool slightly. Tip into a small food processor and add all

the other ingredients. Grind and pulse until you have a paste that is fully emulsified and super-smooth.

Pour into two small, lidded containers, smooth the surface and trickle over a little extra sesame oil, to preserve the surface. Put in the fridge, where the paste will keep happily for anything up to 1 month. Or, you could freeze one of them, if you like.

Puy lentil salad with piquant vegetable vinaigrette

It is just about possible to chop the solid ingredients together in a food processor, but hand-prepared will give a more even texture; food processors have a habit of missing some bits.

Serves 4 as a first course or accompaniment, or 2 as a hearty main dish

250g Puy lentils, washed
2 tbsp finely chopped carrots
2 tbsp finely chopped red pepper
2 tbsp finely chopped spring onion
2 garlic cloves, peeled and finely chopped
2 tbsp finely chopped gherkins (use crisp cornichons)
2 tbsp finely chopped green olives
2 tsp finely chopped capers
2 tbsp red wine vinegar
4–5 tbsp extra virgin olive oil
salt and freshly ground pepper
3 hard-boiled large eggs, finely chopped
2 heaped tbsp chopped flat-leaf parsley

Cook the lentils in about 500ml water until tender; do not add salt. Meanwhile, in a bowl, mix all the rest of the salad ingredients together, except the eggs and parsley. Drain the lentils and allow them to cool slightly for a few minutes.

Tip the lentils into a bowl and add the vegetable vinaigrette. Stir together well, season generously and pile onto a serving dish. Scatter with the chopped eggs and parsley and eat warm or at room temperature.

My dhal

Depending upon how sloppy or thick you like your dhal, I have given a moveable amount of water to play with. At any time during the cooking process, more water may be added, but it is best that you use hot water from a boiled kettle – to keep the temperature even during cooking.

Although it is not essential to soak the moong dhal, I think it cooks more consistently if it is pre-soaked.

Serves 2–3

250g moong dhal, soaked overnight in cold water
1 tbsp turmeric
1–1.5 litres water
75ml oil or ghee
1 tbsp cumin seeds
2 tsp black mustard seeds
1 onion, peeled and finely chopped
4 garlic cloves, peeled, crushed and chopped
2 large tomatoes, peeled and finely chopped
1 small carrot, peeled and grated
250ml coconut milk
coarsely chopped coriander to finish (optional)

Drain the soaked moong dhal, place in a cooking pot or heavy-bottomed pan, add the turmeric and pour on the 1 litre water; do not add salt. Bring to the boil and cook for about an hour until tender.

In a separate pan, heat the oil or ghee until hot. Add the cumin and mustard seeds and briefly fry until popping. Tip in the onion and garlic and fry until a rich golden colour. Add to the dhal and stir in.

Season with salt and pepper to taste and then add the tomatoes, carrot and coconut milk. Simmer all together very gently for about 20 minutes until the carrot is thoroughly cooked through. Serve in warmed bowls, with some chopped coriander sprinkled on top, if you like.

Baked barley 'pilaf' with Provençal vegetables

A colourful, jewel-like assembly with the lovely flavours of a ratatouille permeating the pulse.

Serves 3–4

250g pearl barley, soaked overnight in cold water
1 large onion, peeled and finely chopped
4–5 tbsp olive oil
4 garlic cloves, peeled and finely chopped
500ml stock
2 bay leaves
2 tsp harissa (optional)
1 small aubergine, diced
1 small green pepper, cored, de-seeded and diced
1 small red pepper, cored, de-seeded and diced
1 medium courgette, diced
2 large, ripe tomatoes, diced
salt and freshly ground pepper

Preheat the oven to 180°C/gas mark 4. Drain the pearl barley, rinse in a sieve and then drain thoroughly.

Using a large, lidded stove-top-to-oven pot, fry the onion in 1 tbsp olive oil until golden. Add the barley and garlic, with a little more olive oil and stir around until well coated. Pour in the stock, add the bay leaves and stir in the harissa, if using. Turn off the heat, cover and put to one side.

Heat a little more olive oil in a large frying pan (preferably non-stick) and briskly fry the aubergine, peppers and courgette until nicely coloured. Add the tomatoes, stir around briefly, then tip all these vegetables into the stock and barley. Bring up to a simmer, put on the lid and bake in the oven for 20–25 minutes. On removing from the oven, do not take off the lid. Leave for 5 minutes.

Now uncover and fluff up the pilaf with a couple of forks. Lay a tea towel over the top, clamp it in place with a lid and leave for a further 5 minutes, to allow any excess steam to be absorbed. Serve on hot plates.

This is delicious eaten with slices of toasted country bread, brushed with olive oil and smeared thickly with fresh garlic purée (see page 90).

White beans, ceps & cream

Make this almost instant dish in cep season (late summer to late autumn), when they are plentiful. Otherwise, frozen ones can be used successfully.

Reconstituted dried ceps (soaked in warm water for 20 minutes), on the other hand, will produce a good dish, but will not contain those deliciously slippery moments of fresh fungi amongst the soft and creamy beans.

Serves 2

2 shallots, peeled and finely chopped
30g butter
1 tbsp dry vermouth
150ml whipping cream
2 garlic cloves, peeled and finely chopped
250g fresh ceps, cleaned and thinly sliced
1 x 400–420g tin of haricot or cannellini beans
1 heaped tbsp chopped parsley
small squeeze of lemon juice
salt and freshly ground pepper
a little freshly grated Parmesan

Using a deep-ish pot, fry the shallots in half the butter until softened and just a little golden. Add the vermouth and allow to sizzle and reduce a little. Pour in the cream and stir in the garlic. Bring up to a simmer, switch off the heat, cover and leave to infuse. Preheat a radiant grill.

In a small frying pan, melt the remaining butter and gently fry the ceps until pale golden and smelling fabulous. Tip into the cream infusion and stir in. Drain the beans in a sieve and rinse with boiling water from a kettle, then shake well until dry. Add the beans, along with the parsley, lemon juice and seasoning to the creamy ceps and heat through.

Tip into a shallow gratin dish. Sprinkle over the Parmesan – not too much, just as a savoury, finishing touch. Place under the grill to glaze for a few minutes. Serve at once, perhaps with a salad of bitter, autumnal leaves.

Savoury sweetcorn pudding

My American friend Betsey Apple supplied me with a recipe for corn pudding. It may have changed almost beyond recognition now, so sorry Betsey, but your recipe is the inspiration for this dish. And thank you very much indeed!

This is delicious eaten with some very ripe tomatoes, skinned, chopped and seasoned, mixed with sliced spring onions and basil, then lubricated with a little excellent wine vinegar and olive oil.

Serves 4

2 very fresh corn cobs, about 450g in total
25g unsalted butter, melted
1 heaped tsp potato flour
150ml milk
150ml double cream
large pinch of ground mace
1 tsp Maldon salt
freshly ground white pepper
3 large egg yolks, well beaten
1 small ball of buffalo mozzarella, drained and cut into small chunks
1–2 tbsp freshly grated Parmesan, plus a little extra to serve if liked

Preheat the oven to 200°C/gas mark 6. Cut the corn cobs in half, then stand upright and cut the kernels from the cobs, using a sharp knife (yield: about 250g kernels). Melt the butter in a saucepan and stew the corn for a few minutes until almost tender.

Slake the potato flour with a little of the milk in a small bowl. Add the rest of the milk and the cream to the corn with the mace and season with the salt and plenty of pepper. Bring up to a gentle simmer and then stir in the slaked potato flour. The mixture will thicken almost immediately, so stir together well and quickly, then remove from the heat. Leave to cool for about 5 minutes, then stir in the beaten egg yolks.

Butter a shallow, 1 litre capacity baking dish and pour in the mixture. Scatter the chunks of mozzarella on top and then, using your fingers, push them under the surface. Sprinkle over the Parmesan and bake in the oven for about 30 minutes.

Lift out from the oven carefully and leave to cool to warm. Serve from the dish, to be spooned out onto warmed plates at the table. Sprinkle over some extra Parmesan, if liked.

Grilled white polenta with fonduta

The fontina cheese needs to be grated and soaked in the milk the night before you want to make it, so do this and make the polenta the day before you wish to eat the dish. Fonduta is closely related to Swiss fondue.

Serves 4

for the polenta
1 litre water
1 tsp salt
175g white polenta (in a bowl)
25g unsalted butter, cubed
about 50g Parmesan, freshly grated
a little olive oil for grilling

for the fonduta
200g fontina cheese, coarsely grated (see below)
200ml milk
75g butter, cubed
3 large egg yolks

to serve
extra freshly grated Parmesan

To cook the polenta, bring the water and salt to the boil in a large, heavy-bottomed pan. Take a solid whisk and begin to stir the water. With your other hand, slowly tip in the polenta in a fine, steady, sand-like stream. Do not stop whisking until all the polenta has been added. Turn down the heat to very low, or preferably place the pan on a heat-diffuser mat, and continue whisking for a few moments.

Change the whisk to a wooden spoon and continue stirring with this. Once the polenta starts to come away from the sides of the pan, it is ready. Pour it into an oiled, straight sided plastic box, ideally, so that, once set, it may easily be slipped out and thickly sliced, ready for grilling. Keep in the fridge until ready to use.

To make the fonduta, put the (soaked) cheese and milk, and the butter in the top half of a double boiler or in a heatproof bowl. Cook over simmering water until the cheese has completely melted. Add the egg yolks one by one, beating each into the mixture until thoroughly blended in. Once incorporated, continue stirring until thickened, glossy and just pourable.

To serve, cut the polenta into slices, about 1.5cm thick. Lightly brush each surface with olive oil and heat a ridged grill or a solid-based frying pan until very hot. Grill the polenta slices until well coloured on each side; this will take a good 5 minutes, or so; I like it quite burnished.

Place two pieces of polenta on each warmed plate and generously spoon over the fonduta. Sprinkle with a little extra Parmesan and eat at once.

RICE

Risotto & Pilaf

Whenever I attempt to diet with a lowering of my carbohydrate intake these days, it will always be rice that I miss most. This wasn't always the case, though, as an understanding of rice cookery is a skill that came rather late to me. Before this, it was potatoes that had left the largest hole of desire, along with all things encased in delicious pastry. Pasta was always lower down this order of regime, but which is not to say that a marvellous, authentically made lasagne doesn't remain as one of my most favourite things to both cook and eat.

All rice cookery I used to attempt always turned out as one great big disappointment to me. There was my water-logged plain-boiled, a risotto with the texture of pudding, and a pudding where the milk seemed completely alien to the rice with which it was intended to bond. Even a simple pilaf eluded me, although I had been precisely instructed by a sweet and friendly, Anglo-Indian cook in my late teens. Because of all this constant failure, it further caused me to dislike eating the stuff, too. A kind of gastro-sulk had firmly set in.

So, it was not until I discovered a method of making pilaf from the exacting words of Madhur Jaffrey, and from one of her earlier books, that I eventually enjoyed some success. Apart from the fact that the amount of liquid used was far less than I had otherwise previously employed, there was also a finishing process that I was ignorant to: the absolute non-removal of the lid of the pot for several minutes after having been taken from the oven, with a further instruction of the laying over a tea towel once the rice had been fluffed up with a fork. I should also add that the brand of basmati rice sold under the name of 'Tilda' always seems to behave better than others. And I never wash Tilda rice, either, even though this preliminary task is thought of as essential by almost everyone.

As far as risotto is concerned, I had it all wrong right from the start. In the early 1980s I was very proud of my risotto using a pre-fluffed (in other words, part-cooked rice), which bears no resemblance to the real thing, be it everyday arborio, or the specialist grains – vialone nano and carnaroli. Well, one lives and learns... And, you know, hardly any of us, then, knew which was the correct rice or had much idea as to how authentic risotti should be fabricated. I eventually turned to the scientifically informed and marvellous Marcella Hazan, who put me straight with her words of wisdom.

It occurs to me, in fact, that the majority of influence over the years has been that of women cookery writers. And how correctly and wonderfully sexist is that?

Tomato risotto

I have always been a stickler for the fat used in making risotto being all about butter. However, it seemed right, here, to use olive oil at the beginning of the process; I think it may have something to do with this one also being all about tomatoes, so synonymous with olive oil. Don't worry, however, there is plenty of butter to come at the end...

Serves 2

- 250g ripe, cherry tomatoes, halved
- 2 garlic cloves, peeled, crushed and finely chopped
- pinch of dried chilli
- salt and freshly ground pepper
- 1 onion, peeled and finely chopped
- 1 tbsp olive oil
- 200g carnaroli rice
- 400–450ml hot stock
- 50g butter
- 1 tbsp dry vermouth
- 1 tbsp freshly grated Parmesan, plus extra to serve

Blend the tomatoes, garlic, chilli and a little salt in a food processor to a very smooth, liquid purée. In a deep-sided, heavy-bottomed pan, fry the onion in the olive oil until softened and pale golden. Tip in the tomatoes and simmer until reduced by half. Add the rice and turn up the heat. Stirring vigorously with a sturdy wooden spoon, allow the rice to soak up the tomato and then add a ladleful of stock. Still stirring, let the rice absorb the stock before adding another ladleful. Continue adding the stock in this way; you may not need all of it.

Stop adding stock when the risotto is looking a lovely, pale orange colour, is sloppily pourable and the rice is starting to become tender and not chalky in the middle (I always keep tasting a grain as I go). Now remove from the heat and quickly beat in the butter. Cover and leave to settle for 5 minutes.

Check for seasoning and vigorously beat in the vermouth and Parmesan. Spoon onto hot plates and hand extra Parmesan at table. For me, when decanted from its cooking pot, the perfect texture of a risotto is that of slow lava.

Buttery pilaf with two onions, coconut & green paste

It is not essential to include the green paste here, but it further perks up this already fragrant pilaf. One of my favourite dishes in this book.

Serves 2

- 1 medium onion, peeled and finely chopped
- 60g butter
- 200g basmati rice (Tilda, for preference)
- 200ml stock
- 125ml coconut milk
- salt and freshly ground white pepper
- 4 thinly pared strips of lemon zest
- 1 tbsp green paste (see page 157), or 2 tbsp chopped coriander
- 2 tbsp finely sliced spring onions (mostly green)
- juice of ½ lemon or lime

Preheat the oven to 180°C/gas mark 4. Using a lidded, stove-top-to-oven pot, fry the onion in half the butter until a rich golden colour. Add the rice, stir it around until well coated with buttery onion and then add the stock, coconut milk, salt, plenty of pepper and the lemon zest. Bring to a simmer, stir once to distribute everything and pop on the lid. Bake in the oven for 15 minutes. On removing from the oven do not take off the lid! Leave to stand for 10 minutes.

Now thoroughly stir in the green paste or coriander, spring onion and the remaining butter. Place a tea towel over the pot, tuck it down inside slightly, clamp it down with the lid and leave, once more, for a further 5 minutes; this allows the rice to further steam, with the towel absorbing any excess, so resulting in a dry and fluffy pilaf. Serve on hot plates and squeeze over the lemon or lime juice.

Congee with bok choy, golden fried garlic, green chilli & soy

Asian savoury rice porridge would be a fairly accurate description, here. Also, it is one of the finest hangover foods I know, although deeply comforting at any time. For a truly authentic taste, try to find Chinese sesame oil, chilli oil and light soy sauce (a superior brand in each case).

Serves 2 for a main dish, or 4 as a first course

125g jasmine rice
1–1.5 litres stock
7 thick slices fresh ginger (unpeeled)
3 tbsp Chinese Shaohsing rice wine
for the garnishes
3–4 bok choy, or similar Chinese greens, steamed until tender, then sliced
4–5 large garlic cloves, peeled, thinly sliced and gently fried in a little oil until pale golden and lightly crisp
2–3 spring onions, trimmed and thinly sliced
shredded fresh ginger, steeped in rice vinegar
2 fresh, large green chillies (generally milder), sliced

to finish
light soy sauce
toasted sesame oil and/or chilli oil

In a large, heavy-bottomed pot, mix together the rice, 1 litre stock and the ginger and bring up to a simmer. Cover and cook very gently indeed (a heat-diffuser mat is helpful), for at least 1 hour or maybe longer, stirring from time to time; the desired consistency should be that of porridge, and where the rice harmoniously marries with the stock as one; you may need more stock to get it just right. As ever, practice makes perfect. (You may also prefer to cook it in a very low oven, covered, but it must be finished on the stove top.)

Naturally, the rice will be overcooked almost to the point of submission. Once you are happy with its consistency, fish out the ginger and discard, then add the rice wine and stir in.

To finish the congee, ladle it into bowls, distribute the garnishes as you see fit, then trickle on a little of the soy and oils.

EGGS

Scrambled & Baked

I remain forever amazed and perplexed – and sometimes quite cross, if the truth be known – that perfectly accomplished cooks are so capable of making a complete hash over scrambling eggs. But, even more bewildering, is that the same person is then also quite happy to sit down and eat them!

The sad little yellow heap is, naturally, going to be woefully overcooked and a pale liquid (usually added milk) will have separated out from the eggs. This seepage, of course, will further soak into a slice of pale, undercooked and flabby toast, upon which these bouncy lumps will just about tumble upon, but with plenty of bits skittering around the plate, too. The cooking receptacle will have been some battered old pan, which is now coated in furry yellow stuff. Someone with whom I once shared a flat, years ago, would then leave a pan such as this to soak for days.

One of the main problems with managing something so inherently simple, is that the preparation is often rushed. As opposed to an omelette, which can – and should – be deftly made in a matter of seconds, scrambled eggs need the exact opposite treatment. In these more modern times since those flat-sharing days, I have discovered that it is well worth investing in a solid-based, non-stick pan.

Apart from the obvious benefits with the ease of washing up later, the non-stick coating of the pan allows a somewhat more evident observation of how the eggs are coming along as they quietly curdle into a mass, easily lifted from the base of the pan as the spoon nudges its way around. It goes without saying that the heat should be tentative.

The finest butter will further enhance the taste of the finest scrambled eggs, although

I do not believe that adding cream improves that which is already going to be a rich assembly. Milk? Well, I am not exactly sure. My mother certainly used to beat some milk into the eggs, but I have always put that down to thrift rather than improvement.

The simplest way to prepare a dish of baked eggs is to break one large or two small eggs into a well-buttered, eared dish, season them and spoon over a couple of tablespoonfuls of cream. Bake for anything from 7 and up to 10 minutes in the oven, at 180°C/gas mark 4, for a runny yolk and a just-set white. Or, you can cook them in a steamer, but the cooking time should be slightly less and the water beneath only at the gentlest simmer.

Practice, as usual, makes perfect, but I do tend to poke them with a tentative finger when I think they are ready, just to see if the white is setting beneath the cream and the surface of the yolk is turning opaque. If you prefer to use small ramekins – the French oeufs en cocottes, in other words – the accuracy of cooking the eggs becomes more difficult to judge, with the bubbling cream above disguising what is going on in this deeper vessel. However, this way has a special charm to it, with nice things happening when spooning into the depths.

Baked eggs with cream, wild garlic & morels

This particular egg dish celebrates that seasonal moment when wild garlic and fresh morels happily coincide. The first asparagus, later in the morel season, is another possible partner for baked eggs.

Naturally, you should use the very freshest, most beautiful eggs you can lay your hands on. Although the quality of the other ingredients is important, it is the eggs, above all, that must shine.

Serves 2

50g butter, plus extra to butter the dishes
12 small fresh morels, briefly rinsed, dried and cut in half lengthways
salt and freshly ground pepper
15–20 wild garlic leaves, stalks removed and sliced into thick ribbons
2 large, or 4 medium, very fresh eggs
4 tbsp double cream

Preheat the oven to 180°C/gas mark 4. Lightly butter 2 shallow, ovenproof dishes. Melt slightly less than half the butter in a frying pan, add the morels, season and lightly fry until tender. Lift out with a slotted spoon and divide between the two buttered dishes.

Return the pan to the heat, add the rest of the butter and cook the wild garlic, also seasoned, until softened and wilted. Spoon into the dishes.

Mix the wild garlic together with the morels and spread towards the edges of the dishes, so making room for the incoming egg(s). Pour 1 tbsp cream into each dish, break in the egg(s), season and then pour on the rest of the cream. Slide into the oven and cook for 7–10 minutes until cooked with a runny yolk and a just-set white. Serve at once.

Scrambled eggs & tomatoes on toast with olive oil & parmesan

I have successfully made these quite delightful scrambled eggs with ripe cherry tomatoes simply whizzed to a smooth purée, skins and cores intact. These normally offending parts become indecipherable and do not spoil the dish in any way, trust me.

Otherwise, use the ripest, larger tomatoes you can find, but if this is the case, peeling and de-seeding is advised. Some shredded basil leaves added at the time of scrambling can be a pleasing, added flavour to the dish. Summer Sunday supper at its finest, I'd say, wouldn't you?

Serves 2

200g cherry tomatoes
1–2 garlic cloves– 1 peeled and crushed to a paste with ½ tsp Maldon salt, 1 halved, to finish (optional)
pinch of dried chilli or freshly ground pepper
1 tbsp extra virgin olive oil, plus a little extra to serve
5 large eggs, beaten
2 slices country or sourdough bread
1½–2 tbsp freshly grated Parmesan

Whiz together the tomatoes, crushed garlic, chilli or pepper and olive oil in a blender or food processor until smooth. Place in a saucepan (preferably non-stick) and allow to reduce over a moderate heat until thick and sauce-like. Tip in the eggs and slowly scramble them with the tomato until done to your liking; I advise just pourable.

Meanwhile, toast the bread. You may like to lightly rub the surfaces with a cut clove of garlic, for more punch. Pile the scrambled eggs and tomatoes onto the toasted bread, sprinkle with Parmesan and trickle over a little more olive oil to serve.

Egg mayonnaise

Very fresh eggs and good, thick home-made mayonnaise are essential here.

Serves 2

3 large eggs (at room temperature)
home-made mayonnaise (see below)
several inner, pale yellow leaves of a traditional round lettuce
1 punnet of mustard cress
4 radishes, trimmed, washed and quartered lengthways
snipped chives
cayenne pepper

To cook the eggs, put them into a pan, cover with cold water and bring up to the boil, then switch off the heat, put on the lid and leave them for 6 minutes to cook in the residual heat. Then, run a cold running tap into the pan for about 3 minutes to halt the cooking. This should achieve a perfectly cooked yolk, with a nicely set, rather than rubbery, white.

To serve, arrange the lettuce leaves on two plates. Shell the hard-boiled eggs and cut in half lengthways. Place 3 halves on each portion of lettuce, then neatly coat with enough mayonnaise to just cover them. Snip the cress to fall around the edges of the eggs and add the radishes here and there. Snip chives over the eggs and sprinkle with cayenne pepper.

Mayonnaise

This is a good, thick mayonnaise, which keeps well in the fridge. It is important to have all the ingredients at room temperature before you start. Don't be frightened of adding all the oil; it will be fully incorporated if you follow the method. Also, for efficiency and ease, I recommend using an electric hand mixer.

Makes about 500ml

2 large egg yolks
2 tsp smooth Dijon mustard
salt and freshly ground white pepper
300ml sunflower or other neutral oil
juice of ½ large lemon
150ml light olive oil

Place the egg yolks in a roomy bowl and mix in the mustard and a little seasoning. Beginning slowly, beat together while very slowly trickling in the neutral oil (I always find that this will emulsify easier than olive oil, for some reason). When the mixture becomes very thick, add a little lemon juice. Continue beating, adding the oil a little faster now and speeding up the beating speed.

Once the neutral oil has been exhausted, add some more lemon juice and then begin incorporating the olive oil. Once this has also been used up, add a final squeeze of lemon juice. Taste for seasoning and you may also like to add a little more lemon juice, if it suits. Pack into a lidded plastic pot and keep in the fridge until ready to use.

Omelette lyonnaise

To add extra texture and deliciousness to the omelette, you may further like to add in some very tiny croûtons just before the omelette is folded over. Without beating about the bush, this is a very buttery, but quite gorgeous omelette.

Serves 1

2 medium onions, about 250g in total, peeled
25g butter, plus an extra
2 thin slices for cooking
the omelette
3 medium eggs
salt and freshly ground pepper
2 tsp finely chopped parsley
2 tsp red wine vinegar

Slice the onions very thinly. Melt the butter in a heavy-bottomed, small saucepan and cook the onions very gently until completely soft and just beginning to turn pale golden; this can take anything up to 30 minutes, so don't rush it and stir regularly. Allow to cool.

Beat the eggs with the seasoning and parsley, then stir in the onions. Melt a slice of butter in your favourite omelette pan and make the omelette in the usual fashion, tipping and tilting the pan so the runny egg finds the bottom of the pan where it may set; a palette knife is useful here.

When the omelette is perfectly cooked, turn it out onto a warm plate, then quickly add the final slice of butter to the pan, cook until nut brown, then pour over the omelette. In the still hot pan, add the vinegar, swirl it around and spoon over the omelette. Eat at once.

Croustade d'oeuf 'Maintenon'

This is based upon a superb dish created by the great Michel Bourdin when he was Chef at The Connaught Hotel, London. The original was made using quail eggs: 'Croustade d'oeufs de cailles Maintenon' was its name, then.

Serves 4

4 very fresh large eggs
splash of malt vinegar

for the pastry

120g plain flour
pinch of salt
90g butter, frozen in a block
2–3 tbsp ice-cold water, mixed with a generous squeeze of lemon juice
a little soft butter for greasing the tins

for the mushroom duxelles

50g butter
4 shallots, peeled and chopped
350g mushrooms, chopped, stalks and all
salt and freshly ground pepper
2 tbsp Madeira
150ml dry white wine
squeeze of lemon juice
2 tsp chopped tarragon

for the hollandaise sauce

3 large egg yolks
splash of water
225g unsalted butter, melted, left to settle in the pan and kept warm
juice of ½ a lemon
salt and freshly ground white pepper

To cook the eggs, put them into a pan, cover with cold water and bring up to the boil, then switch off the heat, put on the lid and leave them for 6 minutes to cook in the residual heat. Then, run a cold running tap into the pan for about 3 minutes to halt the cooking. This should achieve a perfectly cooked yolk, with a nicely set, rather than rubbery, white.

To serve, arrange the lettuce leaves on two plates. Shell the hard-boiled eggs and cut in half lengthways. Place 3 halves on each portion of lettuce, then neatly coat with enough mayonnaise to just cover them. Snip the cress to fall around the edges of the eggs and add the radishes here and there. Snip chives over the eggs and sprinkle with cayenne pepper.

Oeufs 'mollet' à l'indienne

I particularly like to serve these eggs upon a bed of rice salad with peas so I have included the recipe here, but you can serve them on their own if you prefer. You will need to have a quantity of curry essence and some home-made mayonnaise to hand.

Serves 4

8 large eggs (at room temperature)
curry essence (see page 79)
about 6 tablespoons home-made mayonnaise (see left)
8 thin strips of cooked pimento, from a jar

for the rice and pea salad

200g basmati rice (Tilda, for preference)
325ml water
1 heaped tsp Maldon salt
150g frozen petit pois
2 tsp groundnut or other neutral oil
25g butter
a light sprinkling of white wine (or tarragon) vinegar
2 spring onions, trimmed and finely chopped
grated zest and juice of ½ lime
1 heaped tbsp chopped mint
freshly ground white pepper

Preheat the oven to 180°C/gas mark 4. For the salad, tip the rice into a small, solid cooking pot that has a tight-fitting lid, add the water and salt, then bring up to a simmer. Tip in the peas, add the oil and butter, stir well and return to a simmer. Put on the lid and cook in the oven for exactly 12 minutes.

On removing from the oven, leave the lid in place and allow to stand for 10 minutes. Now, sprinkle over the vinegar, fluff up the rice with a fork, lay a tea towel over the pan and clamp it down with the lid. Leave for another 5 minutes. Tip out onto a tray to cool slightly. Add the rest of the ingredients, seasoning with plenty of pepper, stir and pile onto a serving dish. Let cool.

To soft-boil the eggs, put them into a pan, cover with cold water and bring up to the boil, then switch off the heat, put on the lid and leave them for 5 minutes to cook in the residual heat. Then, run a cold running tap into the pan for about 3 minutes to halt the cooking. This should achieve a perfectly soft-boiled yolk, with a nicely set white. Carefully peel the eggs and place on the rice and pea salad.

Add the curry essence by degrees to the mayonnaise until you are happy with the taste. Spoon over the eggs and decorate each one with a strip of pimento laid diagonally, lengthways.

Savoury cheese custard with cream & chives

'Ethereal' might be an apt description, here, if not too presumptuous – or pretentious, even.

Serves 4

25g butter, melted, to grease the moulds
75g Gruyère, grated
40ml milk
150ml double cream
salt and freshly ground white pepper
3 large egg yolks
2 large whole eggs
1–2 tbsp freshly grated Parmesan

for the cream and chive sauce

150ml whipping cream
50g butter
1 tbsp finely chopped chives
salt and freshly ground pepper

Chill 4 dariole moulds (preferably non-stick), about 150ml capacity. Preheat the oven to 150°C/gas mark 2. Brush the inside of the chilled moulds with the melted butter and put back into the fridge.

Put the Gruyère, milk and cream into a pan over a very gentle heat to melt the cheese, stirring constantly with a wooden spoon until smooth. Season to taste and then strain through a very fine sieve into a bowl. Chill well in the fridge.

Once the mixture is cold, beat in the egg yolks and whole eggs and pass once more through a fine sieve. Fill the buttered moulds with this mixture and stand them in a deep baking tray. Surround with lukewarm water to come two-thirds of the way up the side of the moulds. Bake on the middle shelf of the oven for 45–50 minutes, or until firm to the touch.

Meanwhile, make the chive sauce. Gently simmer the cream and butter together for 3–4 minutes until lightly thickened. Whisk vigorously until homogenised; keep warm.

Remove the timbales from the oven and leave them to rest for 5 minutes. Preheat a radiant grill.

Now carefully run a small knife around the edge of the moulds and then gently invert into 4 lightly buttered, individual, shallow ovenproof dishes. Carefully sprinkle the surfaces of the timbales with the Parmesan, allowing a little to trail down the sides. Flash under the grill briefly, to gild them. To serve, stir the chives into the sauce and pour around the timbales. Eat without delay.

Pene's celebrated cheese soufflé

My friend Pene cooks the best cheese soufflé. She and her husband, Albert, like to eat this little beauty for supper after having enjoyed a long lunch out. Having experienced such an occasion with them as their guest, I can only say how very sensibly some folk plan their day.

Serves 4

40g butter, plus extra to butter the dish
25g plain flour
200ml semi-skimmed milk
4 large egg yolks
5 large egg whites
150g mature Cheddar, grated
25g Gruyère, grated
25g Parmesan, finely grated, plus a little extra to finish
salt
generous pinch of cayenne pepper

Preheat the oven to 200°C/gas mark 6. Thoroughly butter an 18cm diameter soufflé dish, about 8cm deep.

Melt the butter in a saucepan and mix in the flour. Cook together for a couple of minutes to make a roux, then gradually whisk in the milk until a smooth, very thick sauce is achieved. Remove from the heat and leave to cool slightly for a couple of minutes, then add the egg yolks one by one, beating them in thoroughly. Stir in the grated cheeses and season with salt and the cayenne. Pour into a roomy bowl, removing every last vestige of the mixture with a rubber spatula.

Whisk the egg whites in another bowl until firm. Stir a small amount into the cheese mixture to slacken it, then deftly fold in the rest of the whites, using a serving spoon or spatula.

Gently pile the mixture into the buttered soufflé dish and sprinkle the surface with extra Parmesan. Bake in the oven for 30–35 minutes, or until well risen, and golden and crusted on the surface.

FRUIT

Blueberries & Blackcurrants

Initially, I wasn't going to include puddings in this book. However, just because the general premise concerns itself with non-carnivorous savoury delights, I felt that you, the reader, should not be deprived of some delightful desserts to finish with – and I love sweet things as much as anyone, both to eat and to cook. The only guideline I gave myself, nonetheless, was to limit the selection to a basis of fruit. I'm not quite sure why, but it just seemed more fitting, that's all.

I know that to munch on raw blueberries is probably the most healthy way of eating ever – or, at least, that is what we have been told by hale and hearty gurus the world over. However, the finest flavour of the blueberry and similar berries of the genus vaccinium – whimberries (most heavily harvested in my home county, Lancashire), bilberries, whortleberries and huckleberries – is when these dark little fruits have been cooked. Sugar and a touch of lemon juice are all that are necessary to bring out their hidden essence, although even I have successfully used a powdered sweetener when feeling chaste.

Henry, a friend with whom I walk twice a week, swears by a large bowl of porridge, early every morning, then showers his serving with raw blueberries.

I tell him that I can think of nothing more disgusting than to mix raw fruit of any kind with hot porridge oats: 'It don't work!', I cry. 'I make this little blueberry compote for my porridge and it is just lovely', I continue. 'Too much of a fag', he says. Each, as ever, to their own, I guess...

Anyway, this compote really is dead simple to prepare: take 200g blueberries, 1 rounded tablespoonful of caster sugar (about half that of sweetener), or to taste, and the juice of half a small lemon. Gently heat in a stainless steel pan until the berries burst and have exuded a modicum of juice. Cool them, or serve warm. The compote keeps well in the fridge for several days, too.

A blackcurrant jelly was on the menu at our restaurant Bibendum, in London, almost every day. It wobbled nicely and was served with crème Chantilly and warm, freshly baked Madeleines. Everyone loved it. I cannot really give the original recipe here, however, as it contains non-vegetarian gelatine and will not turn out exactly the same when made with agar flakes. However, when set with this seaweed-based gelling agent, it does work as a wonderful, fruit layer in a recipe for trifle (see page 202).

Blueberry pie

Generally, when making a traditional, English fruit pie (pastry both below and above), one does not add anything else to the filling except the fruit, sugar and maybe a spice flavour, say. In contrast, an American fruit pie almost always includes a modicum of thickener (cornflour here, cornstarch over there), and several flecks of butter, too . I have, of late, warmed most generously to these new additions, as they add, respectively, both a pleasing extra richness and also prevent excess juice from pouring out of the pie while it cooks – as my Mother's, although quite delicious whimberry pie, used to do all over the bottom of the oven.

Serves 4

for the pastry
65g cold, unsalted butter, diced
65g cold vegetable shortening (i.e. Trex), diced
200g plain flour
pinch of salt
2–3 tbsp ice-cold water, to mix
a little milk for brushing

for the filling
2 tbsp lemon juice
1 rounded tbsp cornflour
75g caster sugar, plus a little extra for sprinkling
500g blueberries
several flecks of unsalted butter

To make the pastry, put the fats, flour and salt into a food processor and briefly process until resembling breadcrumbs. Add enough water to form a dough and mix until well amalgamated. Knead lightly and chill in the fridge for at least 30 minutes. Cut off one-third of the dough for the lid (weigh the pastry, for accuracy) and re-wrap. Roll out the larger piece to a 2–3mm thick circle.

Preheat the oven to 200°C/gas mark 6 and place a baking sheet inside to heat up. Lightly grease a 20cm loose-bottomed tart tin, 4cm deep, and line with the pastry circle, allowing a little overhang. Prick the base several times with a fork.

For the filling, whisk together the lemon juice, cornflour and 75g sugar in a large bowl until smooth. Add the blueberries and turn all together with a spatula, until the berries are well coated. Tip this into the pastry case and allow to settle. Disperse the butter flecks over the surface.

Roll out the other piece of pastry to a 2mm thick circle. Brush the edge with a little milk and then flip the pastry over the filling to form a lid. Tuck down around the outside of the fruit and press the edge onto the rim of the pastry base to form a seal. Trim off excess pastry with a sharp knife.

Brush the surface with milk and press the tines of a fork around the pastry edge – for prettiness as much as anything. Make 3 small cuts in the centre of the pie to allow steam to escape and sprinkle the surface generously with caster sugar.

Slide the pie onto the baking sheet in the oven and bake for 10 minutes, then turn the temperature down to 180°C/gas mark 4. Bake the pie for another 30–40 minutes or until the surface is nicely crusted and golden. Serve at warm-to-room temperature for maximum enjoyment – and with very cold pouring cream, too.

Blackcurrant jelly trifle

I have used agar flakes here, to fulfil the vegetarian option. If you would like to make the original jelly, you will find it in an earlier cookery book of mine, Gammon & Spinach.

Serves 6

for the blackcurrant jelly
300ml water
4 tsp agar flakes
500g fresh or frozen blackcurrants
250g caster sugar
175ml port

for the other trifle layers
12 amaretti biscuits (i.e. 12 halves)
2 tbsp crème de cassis
2 tbsp port
1 tbsp Cognac
400ml whipping cream
½ vanilla pod, split lengthways
3 large egg yolks
1 large egg
1 rounded tbsp caster sugar

to finish
300ml double cream
1 tbsp icing sugar
silver balls and angelica (optional)

To make the jelly, put the water into a stainless steel pan and sprinkle over the agar flakes. Stir in and leave to soften for 5 minutes, then add the blackcurrants, sugar and port. Bring up to a low simmer, cover and cook for 10 minutes. Tip into a sieve suspended over a bowl. Leave to drain and drip for 30 minutes or so, then gently press upon the fruit with the back of a ladle to extract any final juices. Pour into 6 deep glass dishes and put in the fridge to set for at least 3–4 hours or overnight, if you like.

Break up the amaretti buscuits into small pieces and mix them with the crème de cassis, Port and Cognac. Allow the alcohols to be soaked up by the biscuits, then carefully spoon them over the surface of the jelly. Put back into the fridge.

To make the custard layer, heat the whipping cream with the vanilla pod, give it a quick whisk to disperse the vanilla seeds, cover and leave to infuse. Beat the egg yolks and egg with the sugar. Strain over the vanilla flavoured cream and mix together. Pour back into the cream pan and cook very gently over a low heat, stirring constantly, until thickened. Be careful of overcooking, however, but be brave, because if the custard is not cooked enough, it will not be firm enough, once cold; you can safely take it as far as the odd blip, and when this happens, whisk vigorously to disperse the hotspots. Strain immediately into a bowl, cover and cool completely.

Put the custard into the fridge to chill and thicken and then spoon over the jelly and biscuits. Return to the fridge for 30 minutes.

Whip the cream with the icing sugar until just holding peaks. Pile on top of the trifle in a swirly way and decorate with the angelica and silver balls, if liked. Chill once more until ready to eat.

Raspberry crumble

I like to serve this crumble in individual, shallow dishes, for best effect.

Serves 2
250g raspberries
sugar for sprinkling
several flecks of butter

for the crumble
75g plain flour
40g lightly salted butter
30g sugar

Preheat the oven to 180°C/gas mark 4. To make the crumble, place all the ingredients in a big, roomy bowl and deftly rub the ingredients together until the mix is rubbled with tiny bits of butter, amongst an otherwise sandy texture.

Divide the raspberries between 2 dishes, sprinkle with a little sugar and dot with a few flecks of butter. Using a spoon, carefully cover with the crumble mixture, but do not be tempted to press it down. Dust with a little extra sugar.

Bake in the oven for 20–25 minutes, or until the crumble topping is pale golden and the raspberry juice is gently bubbling. Serve warm, rather than piping hot.

Orange brûlée

Do not be concerned that I have listed the crème fraîche as a weight, rather than a volume amount, as such a thick dairy product is always easier to weigh, rather than measure as a liquid – especially if you have one of those flat, digital scales, whereby the measurement can be accurately added to the vessel one is using. That which is even more convenient, is when the cream is sold in 200g cartons...

Serves 4
finely pared zest of
1 large orange (no pith whatsoever)
125g caster sugar
400ml freshly squeezed orange juice, strained
6 large egg yolks
200g crème fraîche

Using a small food processor, grind together the orange zest and 75g of the sugar, until you have a bright orange paste.

Put the orange juice into a stainless steel pan, add the orange zest paste, bring up to a simmer and reduce by half, to about 225ml. Put to one side to cool for 15 minutes.

Whisk the egg yolks and crème fraîche together in a bowl, then whisk in the reduced orange mixture. Return to the pan and cook very gently over a low heat until thickened to a custard-like consistency. Take care to avoid overcooking, but make sure the custard is cooked enough, otherwise it will not be firm enough, once cold; you can safely take it as far as the odd blip, and when this happens, whisk vigorously to disperse the hotspots.

Strain the custard immediately into 4 ramekins and cool completely, then chill in the fridge for at least 6 hours, preferably overnight.

Sprinkle the remaining sugar over the surface of the custards and caramelise under a preheated hot grill, or using a cook's blow-torch, until melted, golden and blistered in parts. Chill once more for 1 hour.

Serve the brûlées very cold. Eat with small teaspoons.

Baked quinces with maple syrup & white pepper

There is a fairly rare eau de vie de coing (French, for quince), of which a small amount may be added to some very cold, lightly sweetened whipped cream, to serve with these delicious quinces.

Serves 2, with seconds
2 quinces, about 600g, washed and quartered lengthways
8 tbsp pure maple syrup
1 tbsp lemon juice
5–6 grindings of white pepper

Preheat the oven to 180°C/gas mark 4. Cut the quinces lengthways into quarters, using a sharp knife. Place in a lidded oven dish, which will accommodate the pieces snugly. Pour over the maple syrup and lemon juice, and grind over the pepper. Mix together with a spoon.

Put on the lid and bake in the oven for about 1 hour, occasionally turning the quinces through the syrup and basting, until they are tender and a gorgeous golden brown colour. Serve warm, with whipped cream flavoured as suggested below, if liked.

Damson & almond sponge pudding

Essentially, deeply dark stewed fruit with a Bakewell pudding top. Outside of the damson season, which is short, substitute plums.

Serves 4

125g butter, softened, plus extra to grease the dish
500g damsons, stoned
100g caster sugar
2 large eggs
1 tsp natural almond extract
100g self-raising flour
50g ground almonds
½ tsp baking powder
pinch of salt
2–3 tsp icing sugar

Preheat the oven to 180°C/gas mark 4. Butter a presentable, fairly deep baking dish, strew with the stoned damsons and cover them with 25g of the butter, in flecks.

In a roomy bowl, beat the rest of the butter together with all the remaining ingredients, apart from the icing sugar, until light and fluffy. Spoon this mixture over the damsons, slide into the oven and bake for 40 minutes. If the surface of the pudding appears to be browning too quickly, turn the oven down to 160°C/gas mark 3.

Sift the icing sugar over the surface and bake for a further 10 minutes, or so, until the sugar melts and becomes slightly crusted and the sponge is gently firm to a touch from the fingers. Leave to cool until warm, then eat with very cold pouring cream.

NUTS & NIBBLES

Nuts & Nibbles

I have given nuts rather less recipe space than anticipated here. More than anything else, this is because of an association with the frightful 'nut cutlet', one of the most infamous vegetarian options of all time. I have always loathed, really loathed the masquerade of manufacturing vegetarian food, then using a moniker normally attached to something very well known indeed which has always been associated with meat products. The 'Vegetarian burger'. Please. 'Vegetarian sausages'. Just go away. Even 'Sausage rolls'. And, of course, that boneless – spineless, actually – 'Nut cutlet'.

A brief reasoning behind this book – although there is more in the introduction – is absolutely not to disguise the fact that to eat happily, healthily and deliciously it is not necessary to eat meat, poultry and fish the majority of time spent at table; the simple reason is to enjoy non-carnivorous dishes, rather than be reminded of a contrary absence.

Nuts, of course, are full of protein – and fat, and carbohydrates, it should also be said – but it is well known that they are a healthy food, if eaten, like all such things, in moderation. Some people, as we know well, may not eat them due to allergy. And so severe can this be that Health and Safety laws now see it as their duty to pronounce on a packet of nuts, that the packet 'contains nuts'. How very efficient and helpful of them to warn us of this impending danger.

For the majority of cocktail party givers, it will always be nuts that the less adventurous host will turn to as 'nibbles' with, perhaps, olives as a secondary gesture to show willing. An astute observation by a comedian on the radio recently opined, however, that 'There are always olives left in bowls the morning after, but all the bowls containing nuts are practically licked clean, so why don't we put out more nuts next time and just forget the olives?' Quite so.

Personally, I love making interesting nibbles and those who eat them (wolf them, actually) are unable to resist, even though this is often preceded by mutterings of 'Oh, I shouldn't, really' and 'My diet is ruined' or, occasionally, 'Yes please! I'm starving!' which is what you really want to hear and is very nice.

Homemade tiny bridge rolls with white truffle paste

'Little soft slippers of eggy white bread with the most sublime and generous filling of white truffle paste smeared within' is how Terence Conran once described the inspiration for these: the panini tartufati offered at Procacci, in Florence. Note that I suggest 'spreadable' Lurpak because if normal butter is used, the rolls, once cold, are firmer than one would wish for. White truffle paste may be purchased from good Italian food shops. To achieve even-sized rolls, it is advisable to weigh the balls of dough.

Enough for about 40 rolls
125ml milk
60g 'spreadable' Lurpak butter
1 tsp Maldon salt
1 ½ tsp sugar
325g strong bread flour
7g sachet easy blend yeast
1 large egg, beaten
to finish the rolls
1 small egg, beaten with a little milk and a pinch of salt

Put the milk, butter, salt and sugar into a pan and heat until just warm to the finger. Put to one side. In a large bowl or electric food mixer, mix together the flour, yeast and beaten egg. Add the milk mixture and blend in with the flour until it has become a dough (occasionally, the mixture is a touch sticky, but once kneading begins, a little extra flour added will rectify this).

Knead for 10 minutes, or so, until nicely soft and supple. Put into a large, lightly greased bowl, cover with a damp tea towel and allow to rise somewhere warm, for about 1 hour, or until doubled in size.

Preheat the oven to 230°C/gas mark 8. Lightly grease a flat baking tray. Tip the risen dough onto a floured surface, punch it down and then knead for a moment or two. Now begin to break off small pieces of dough that weigh 15g each, and set them to one side until all the dough is exhausted.

Form the pieces of dough into little balls, then roll these into tiny torpedo shapes; i.e. slightly higher in the middle than they are at each end, and with a smooth top. As you shape each one, place on the baking tray, spacing them about 2cm apart (once they have risen, they should just be touching each other). Cover with a light and flimsy dry tea towel and, once again, place somewhere warm, to rise for a second time for around 40 minutes, or until more than doubled in size, this time.

Now then, for the brave of heart, this is the time you very lightly brush them with the beaten egg/milk/salt mixture. Occasionally, the rolls are so well risen and light, that the merest touch can maddeningly deflate them. If you are at all nervous about this, then brush them before they rise; the finished result will not be quite as beautiful looking, but at least you will have them perfectly baked!

Anyway, whichever route you take, bake for about 8 minutes on an upper shelf of the oven, but not the top-most one, until golden on top and smelling absolutely wonderful. Cool on a wire rack.

Split lengthways, spread with unsalted butter and slather with truffle paste. Sandwich back together and eat with a glass of the finest white wine you can afford. Finally, do try to eat all of them at their very best – on the day of baking.

Potato fritters with sesame & pine kernels

Offer these either as a small nibble, or as a dish in themselves with, say, a salad of fine green beans.

Makes about 20

500g potatoes (Desiree, for preference), peeled and cut into chunks

for the choux paste

100ml water
25g butter
salt and freshly ground white pepper
50g plain flour
2 large eggs
1 large egg yolk

to finish

flour for coating
1 egg, loosely beaten
2–3 tbsp sesame seeds
3–4 tbsp pine kernels
oil for deep-frying

Steam the potatoes until tender, then allow to dry out a little. Pass them through a mouli légumes (vegetable mill), or potato ricer, onto a sheet of greaseproof paper or a tray. Leave to cool.

Meanwhile, make the choux paste: boil together the water, butter and seasoning in a saucepan. Take off the heat, tip in the flour all at once and beat together, using a wooden spoon, until thoroughly combined and very smooth. Now, one by one, start to beat in the eggs, making sure that each egg has been fully incorporated before adding the next one. The final result should be a glossy, stiff yellow paste. Beat this thoroughly into the dry potato until smooth. Spread into a shallow dish, cover with cling film and put into the fridge to firm up.

Using floured hands or 2 teaspoons, take small amounts of the mixture and form into balls the size of a small-ish walnut. Roll them in flour and put onto a tray. Mix together the sesame seeds and pine kernels and spread them out onto another tray. Now pass each potato ball through beaten egg and then roll them through the seeds and nuts, making sure of a good covering.

Heat the oil in the deep fryer to 170°C and cook the fritters in 2 or 3 batches for about 3–4 minutes, until crisp and golden. Keep warm in a very low oven, on double folded kitchen paper, while you continue with the next batch. Very good eaten with mayonnaise that has had some chilli sauce stirred into it.

Caerphilly cheese croquettes

Best served warm.

Makes about 12–15

150g Caerphilly cheese, grated
200g fresh white breadcrumbs
2 tbsp finely chopped spring onion
3 large egg yolks
1 tbsp chopped parsley
1 tsp mustard powder
salt and freshly ground pepper
a little cream or milk (if needed)
oil for deep-frying
flour for coating
1 large egg, loosely beaten

Mix together the cheese, 100g of the breadcrumbs and spring onion. In a bowl, whisk the egg yolks, parsley, mustard and seasoning together and add the breadcrumb and cheese mixture to make a firm paste; if the mix is too sloppy, add a little more breadcrumbs; if too dry, add a little cream or milk. Form into little cork shapes and place on a floured tray. Put in the fridge to firm up for about an hour.

When ready to cook, heat the oil for deep-frying in a suitable pan to about 170°C. Put the flour, the beaten egg and the remaining breadcrumbs into 3 separate shallow dishes. Firstly, roll the croquettes in flour, then egg and, finally, breadcrumbs. Deep-fry in the hot oil for 3–4 minutes, or until a pale golden colour and nice and crisp. Drain on kitchen paper and serve.

'Ajo verde'

Generally, I am loathe to mess around with aged tradition, but I have here taken the liberty of turning the cold Spanish garlic and almond soup, ajo blanco, into one that is pale green, sweet, and lightly spiced with a little green chilli. I hope you like it. Modestly, I happen to think it is revelatory. Very good as a summer nibble when served in iced shot glasses.

Serves 2–3

- 150g pistachios (skinned, if you can find them)
- 75ml extra virgin olive oil, plus a trickle to serve
- 175g seedless green grapes
- ½ small cucumber, about 125g, peeled and chopped
- 350ml water
- 5–6 garlic cloves, peeled and crushed
- 1½ tsp Maldon salt
- 1 green chilli, de-seeded and chopped
- 10 mint leaves
- 3–4 tsp sherry vinegar, or to taste
- juice of 1 small lime
- croûtons to serve
- 2 ice cubes

In a non-stick frying pan, lightly toast the pistachios in 1 tsp of the oil, colouring them hardly at all. Leave to cool, then tip into a blender. Add all the other ingredients and process until very smooth indeed, then pass through a fine sieve into a bowl, pressing down on the solids to extract every last vestige of liquid.

Chill thoroughly in the fridge for at least 4 hours. Serve in chilled soup bowls, and with super-crisp tiny croûtons. I also like to add one cube of ice to each serving and a tiny trickle of best olive oil, too.

Rachel Cooke's wonderful Parmesan biscuits

I first tasted these extraordinarily delicious biscuits at Rachel and her husband Tony's north London home. They were served with an equally delicious bottle of Champagne, which, in turn, preceded a dinner of a familiar spiced aubergine salad, with a very fine roast chicken to follow. These occasional dinners with particular friends revolve around the consumption of a few fine bottles. So, some excellent red wine was poured, we moved on to slices of ripe cheese... and, at that moment, I felt that all was really quite alright with the world. Silly old Hop.

Makes about 25–30

100g cold, unsalted butter, cut into chunks
100g plain flour
pinch of salt
pinch of cayenne pepper
½ heaped tsp mustard powder
50g mature Cheddar, finely grated
50g Parmesan, finely grated, plus a little extra to finish
1 large egg, beaten

Preheat the oven to 180°C/gas mark 4. Put the butter and flour into a food processor, together with the salt, cayenne pepper, mustard powder and cheeses. Briefly process all together to begin with, and then, finally, pulse the mixture in short spurts as you notice the mixture coming together – as pastry, if you like. Once the texture is clearly 'clumpy', tip it all out onto a lightly floured surface and deftly, but thoroughly, knead it together until well blended and smooth. Wrap in cling film and chill in the fridge for at least 30 minutes.

Gently roll out the pastry on a lightly floured work surface to about a 2mm thickness. Using a 3–5cm pastry cutter, cut out biscuits the size you wish for, depending on the occasion. Lay them out onto a greased baking tray about 2cm apart; it may be necessary to bake them in 2 batches.

Carefully brush the surface of each biscuit with beaten egg and sprinkle over a little finely grated Parmesan. Bake in the oven for 10 minutes, or until a gorgeous, pale golden colour is achieved; the superb smell will also inform you that they are ready. Carefully lift off the tray using a palette knife and place on a cooling rack. Serve while still just warm if possible.

French 75 & Other Cocktails

In my view it is Italian bartenders, and most often on their home ground, who make the finest, most pure and traditional cocktails anywhere. These genial, knowing fellows also present themselves most elegantly in their pressed white linen jackets, black trousers and with brilliant white shirts and thin black (not bow) ties. They are a lesson to all would-be practitioners of the art of mixing a good drink.

One feels relaxed and confident when observing such people at work, rather than becoming stressed, as I do, sitting on my stool and watching the simplest cocktail go from bad to worse in a matter of minutes, even in the heart of London's Mayfair.

The pretty and, I modestly think, delicious Hoppy's Pink is my only real attempt at cocktail creation, here, with the other ones merely touched by personal interpretation. The drink has its origins in the Pink Gin, which was particularly popular in the British Navy pre-and-post the Second World War, but which has now almost disappeared without trace. This is due, of course, to a slew of the filthiest, over-complicated cocktails ever offered to the serious barfly in modern times. Why, pray, would you ever wish to add chocolate to a Martini?

Anyways, as they might say in the more louche bars of Manhattan, this pink drink is a lovely, if potent, early evening summer cocktail. If you wish, a small splash of Campari gives the drink an even pinker colour and also adds a pleasing touch of bitterness.

Firstly, however, here is a classic – and relatively new to me, I might add. First imbibed in the Bar Hemingway of the Paris Ritz.

French 75

Alternatively, as a long drink, in summertime, serve over ice in highball glasses and garnish with a sprig of mint.

Makes 2 drinks
75ml gin (Plymouth, ideally)
75ml lemon juice, strained
3–4 tsp caster sugar
several ice cubes
non-vintage Champagne, chilled

Using a long spoon, mix together the gin, lemon juice, sugar and ice cubes in a jug and stir well. Strain into 2 large, chilled flutes and top up with Champagne.

Jalapeño bloody Mary

The tomato juice needs to be infused with the chillies at least 24 hours in advance. You can, of course, use my vegetarian version of Worcestershire sauce (see page 75).

Makes 2 drinks
300ml tomato juice
2–3 jalapeño chillies, roughly chopped
plenty of ice cubes
75ml vodka
50ml dry sherry
2 tsp Worcestershire sauce
1 tsp Tabasco
juice of 1 small lime
large pinch of celery salt

Having infused the tomato juice with the chillies (see below), strain the juice through a sieve into an ice-filled jug and add everything else. Stir well and strain into small, chilled tumblers.

Correct Pimms

I absolutely loathe Pimms when it resembles fruit salad. This is not that.

Makes 1 moderate jugful, enough for 2–3, depending on thirst...
120ml Pimms No. 1
60ml gin (Plymouth, ideally)
3–4 orange slices
3–4 lemon slices
4–5 mint sprigs
2–3 borage sprigs (optional)
3–4 long strips of cucumber skin
300ml lemonade, chilled
plenty of ice cubes

Mix everything together well in a jug, leave to infuse for 2–3 minutes, then pour into glasses containing more ice. Garnish each glass with mint and an extra slice of orange and lemon, if desired.

Hoppy's pink

My singular attempt at cocktail creation.

Makes 2 drinks
75ml gin or vodka
4–5 drops Angostura bitters
1–2 tsp caster sugar, to taste
100ml freshly squeezed pink grapefruit juice, strained
ice cubes
200ml pink Champagne, chilled
1 pink grapefruit slice, halved

Using a jug, briefly mix together the gin or vodka, bitters, sugar and grapefruit juice, over ice. Strain into 2 large wine glasses, with 5 cubes of ice in each. Top up with Champagne, stir carefully, add the sliced grapefruit and serve promptly.

Index